Let Go of the Rope:
Create Unlimited Confidence
in 3 Simple Steps

By Diana Rogers Jaeger

To every person who wants to create a better future for themselves.

A special dedication to my larger-than-life family and to Kevin, Aiden, and Axl, my favorite adventure buddies.

A portion of the proceeds from the sale of this book supports Girl Scouts, a non-profit organization dedicated to building girls of courage, confidence, and character, who make the world a better place.

Published by CLC Publishing, LLC.
Mustang, OK 73064

Printed in the United States of America

ISBN: 9798864570821

TABLE OF CONTENTS

Find Those Yeses
Create a Persona
Use Your Voice
View the World With Optimism
Have a Difficult Conversation
Make a Power Playlist

INTRODUCTION

A single moment can change you forever.

A powerful experience opens your mind to a new way of seeing and believing. The memory of it never leaves you. It shapes you into the person you become.

Imagine yourself at a mountain retreat. You're new to the camp experience and haven't tried most of the outdoor activities they offer. One day, your group gets into a van to drive to an outdoor rock climbing location in a national forest. You've never gone rock climbing before, and it looks scary.

You hang back and let the other campers go first. It looks challenging for them, and they are a lot taller and bigger than you. You feel intimidated because you're not muscular.

"I'm not strong enough," you think to yourself.

The rock climbing coach walks up to you and asks you to give it a try. You're hesitant, but you go ahead and put on the harness and helmet and listen to instructions.

You're now clipped into the rope. It's time for you to give it a try.

You look at the rock wall directly in front of you, take a deep breath and give the rock climbing commands you learned.

"On belay?" you ask.

"Belay on," your coach replies.

You take a step forward.

"Climbing!" you shout nervously.

"Climb on!" your coach shouts back.

You search the rock surface with your eyes and hands for something to grab. You find two handholds and step up on a tiny ledge sticking out of the rock. You've made it a foot off the ground! You keep repeating the process of finding handholds and footholds and slowly inch your way up the giant rock face.

When you make it several feet off the ground, your coach tells you to "Let go!" It's important that you experience what it feels like to "fall" and have the rope catch you. But you really don't want to let go. Naturally, you're terrified to fall backwards into thin air.

But this is your decision. It's up to you. Do you let fear paralyze you, or do you take the next step?

You decide to trust your coach's expertise and experience. Your fingers slowly let go of the rock and immediately grab the rope as if your life depended on it. You fall with a jerk and bounce up and down in your harness. What a rush! You're dangling in mid-air, but you're completely safe.

You catch your breath and wait for your heartbeat to slow down. After a few minutes, your coach encourages you to let go of the rope and reattach yourself to the rock. You don't want to. Once again, you're afraid to let go. The rope is your lifeline...your safety net...

Then you hear your coach tell you:

"You can't climb if you're holding on to the rope. You have to let go."

This story is real. It's me at nine years old, rock climbing for the very first time. The rock climbing coach is my adopted father. It's a single moment that changed me forever. It's where my confidence journey began.

That summer, my family lived at a Phillips University Science Camp in the San Juan Mountains of Colorado, where my father worked as the camp manager. My siblings and I helped by cleaning cabins, cooking, and washing dishes. We also participated in all the fun camp activities, including backpacking, whitewater rafting, and, of course, rock climbing.

I was always the shortest and skinniest kid in my class. I weighed about 50 pounds and was so tiny that I couldn't fit into a regular-sized harness. My father had to make one for me out of climbing webbing straps.

"I'm just a little girl" was how I defined myself.

But after rock climbing and having the courage to let go of the rope, I would never think of myself that way again.

My father was right. If I remained in the same position gripping the rope for dear life, I couldn't keep climbing. I would have to be lowered down. I definitely didn't want that. I wanted to make it all the way to the top. I may have been a scared little girl, but I was no quitter.

I reluctantly moved my hands from the rope back to the rock, where I found new handholds and footholds. I was rock climbing again! As I did so, my father kept praising me, reassuring me, and coaching me.

Many of his tips were helpful.

"Use your legs! They're stronger than your arms."

Some were not helpful to me at all.

"Pretend the rope isn't there!"

The rope is inches in front of my face and keeping me alive. I didn't want to pretend it wasn't there!

I had many starts and stops. When I was out of breath and my fingers and muscles needed a break, I felt comfortable letting go and sitting in my harness to rest. During those moments when I was 20 to 40 feet off the ground, I took the time to take in my progress and enjoy the view – the clear blue sky, the unique rock formations, the pine trees, and the people far below me on the ground.

I earned this view. Me, myself, and I. My tiny arms and legs climbed and pulled their way up to this very spot. It was a lovely view, but I wanted to see the view from the top.

With each step up, I could see the top getting closer and closer. When I couldn't hear my father's words clearly anymore because he was too far below me, I listened to myself. Because I had made it this far, I felt different, and my thoughts of "I can't" changed to thoughts of "I will."

"I'll show everyone what I can do."

"Size doesn't matter."

"I am strong."

By believing in myself, I made it all the way to the top—70 feet above the ground!

But the thing that climbed the highest that day was my self-confidence.

That day I overcame my self-limiting beliefs about being a girl, my body size, and my capabilities. I rewrote the story I had been telling myself.

Short does not mean weak. Skinny does not mean weak. Girl does not mean weak.

Fear can be misleading. Had I listened to my fears, I would have missed out on a fantastic life-changing experience. On top of that, I got a taste of the rewards that come from taking risks—fun, thrill, self-empowerment, and self-respect.

I felt good about myself and my ability to overcome challenges. At that point in my life, I really needed that. I had experienced my biological father's death and moved halfway across the world from the Philippines to the United States. I was learning a new language and culture. My siblings and I were adopted and became part of a new family. My life had been turned upside down. Without confidence, I believe the trauma and loss I experienced would have had a permanent negative effect on my self-identity.

Rock climbing kick-started my confidence. That day, I saw myself as the actor of my life instead of life acting upon me. I want you to see yourself the same way.

LET GO OF THE ROPE

Like rock climbing, many first-time experiences feel scary and dangerous even when they're not. It feels like the risk of falling isn't worth it and that you're better off not trying. So, you stay put. You stick with what you know and with what feels safe and secure.

Beginner rock climbers feel extremely scared because everything is brand new. They don't know what they are doing yet, and they don't trust themselves or the equipment. Fear of falling and getting hurt is all they can think about, and it's difficult for them to think logically.

A natural response for most people is to cling to the rope with both hands. The rope is their comfort zone. They believe holding on to it will prevent them from falling and hurting themselves. However, they are already safe. The rope, the harness, and the person belaying them have their safety under control. They have to be willing to trust the system and trust themselves. Holding onto the rope only keeps them stuck in the same place. They must choose to let go, get on the rock, and use their hands and feet to climb.

Rock climbing is a great metaphor for life.

 To get to the top you have to leave your comfort zone and let go of the rope.

The rope could be anything – your past, your fear, your insecurities, your beliefs, and anything else that is keeping you from living the life you want.

This book will coach you on how to create confidence from the inside out. I want you to have the confidence to let go of the rope. I want you to take a chance on something that feels scary and see where your climb takes you.

Your journey to confidence begins right now!

You have hopes and dreams of what your life could be. You have a gift the world needs and that you were meant to share with others. Confidence gives you the mindset and the positive energy to show the world what that is and to take actions that turn your dreams into reality.

Without confidence, dreams die. Confidence combats the three major buckets of negative energy that hold people back: fear, uncertainty, and criticism.

People with confidence don't feed their fears and self-doubt. Their focus stays on their vision of what they want to accomplish and the behaviors that will get them closer to achieving that vision.

 There is light in each person, and confidence makes that light shine at full strength.

Confidence is a lifestyle that leads to greater overall happiness and puts its owner on an upward trajectory. People with confidence create their own opportunities by trusting themselves, taking risks, and believing that things will work out.

While others are drowning in toxic self-talk, those with confidence enjoy an inner peace that comes from pursuing a life according to their values. They walk their own path towards their vision.

In their daily lives, they give their attention to people and thoughts that lift them up toward their purpose. They refuse to be weighed down by the mental and emotional weight of past mistakes, negative experiences, and what other people might think.

Like a rocket breaking free from the Earth's gravitational pull, confidence fuels people to leave their comfort zone and shoot for the stars by pursuing their goals and dreams. They've done the work necessary to cast off the fears and insecurities that were holding them down. They feel free to follow their purpose and live life according to their own values.

 Confidence is a superpower that allows you to accomplish things you never thought possible.

Are you ready to experience the clarity and freedom that will set you free to go after what you want?

Are you ready to feel like you're in control of your life?

Are you ready to stop second-guessing yourself and start living life with unlimited confidence?

INSIDE-OUT CONFIDENCE

There are different ways people think about confidence. It's someone who stands up tall and makes direct eye contact. It's someone who feels comfortable in their own body. It's someone who commands attention as a public speaker.

In truth, confidence isn't about looking or acting a certain way. Having a polished look or using powerful body language can be signs of a confident person, but they do not by themselves create or define a confident person.

Some people believe in "fake it until you make it." They want others to perceive them as confident even when they don't feel confident inside. While being perceived as confident can lead to greater credibility and higher social standing, faking confidence makes a person feel like a fake. It's not a long-term strategy.

It's not enough to be perceived as confident. Your goal is to BE confident and to feel, think, and act confidently.

 Self-confidence starts from the inside out.

No suit, no make-up, no weight loss program, nor any item you can buy or consume will give you the type of confidence that transforms your life. The confidence to accept yourself. The confidence that transforms your daily thoughts and behaviors into a positive force. The larger-than-life confidence that kicks open doors of opportunity instead of waiting for them to happen.

I know you believe that a better life exists for you than the one you are living. There is something you really want. Something has been on your mind and in your heart for a while, but you haven't done what you need to make it come true.

Not pursuing your goals and dreams leads to a life filled with guilt and regret, feelings that are a heavy burden to live with day after day. Unless you make different choices, your life will be mediocre and half-lived. That is unacceptable when you are capable of so much more.

Are you ready for a type of confidence that is transformational and long-lasting?

Let Go of the Rope:

Diana Rogers Jaeger

WHAT THIS BOOK WILL DO FOR YOU

Life is short. I'm a person who wants to see progress and results in an efficient amount of time. I blame it on the impatient bone somewhere in my body. Because those things are important to me, and I'm sure they are to you too, I've developed a process that helps people create strong, unlimited confidence in the most direct way possible. Everyone's time, energy, and resources are valuable and should never be wasted.

My goal is to get you from being full of self-doubt to being full of self-confidence in the shortest amount of time.

Most people have never been taught the building blocks to confidence and how it is created. I will lay out three simple steps that will show you how to grow and maintain a high level of self-confidence. Follow these steps, and the outside world will no longer have you second-guessing your self-worth or abilities. You won't need the approval, acceptance, or attention of others to feel good about yourself. You'll be able to bounce back from criticism and mistakes. It will be possible because your confidence will come from within you.

You will learn strategies and techniques for building confidence that lasts. When something does cause your confidence to dip because you are human after all, you will know how to build it back strong each and every time.

 You will possess the knowledge and the power to create unlimited confidence.

DOUBTS AND FEARS ARE NORMAL

When something is new or challenging, your fears kick in and do their best to take over your rational thoughts and behaviors. Your fears want to stop you from doing anything different that may lead to negative experiences such as failure, loss, and pain. It's a form of self-preservation to make you feel "safe."

Fear gets inside your head and asks questions that will make you afraid to take a single step forward.

What if you're not good enough and you fail?

What if you get hurt?

What if people make fun of you?

Everyone experiences doubts and fears because we are all human. Even one of the world's most famous painters, Vincent Van Gogh, struggled with self-doubt during his career.

Despite his inner critic, Van Gogh found a way to create masterpiece after masterpiece. How did he overcome self-doubt? What spurred him to action?

"If you hear a voice within you saying, 'You are not a painter,' then by all means paint, boy, and that voice will be silenced."

– VINCENT VAN GOGH

 Do not let fear and self-doubt dictate the choices that you make.

You can find a way to move past them. Instead of asking yourself, "What if...?", ask yourself, "What next?" Instead of asking yourself, "What if it goes wrong?", ask yourself, "What if it goes right?"

I have definitely experienced doubts and fears throughout my life. One example is wondering if the business I started would make it past its first year. I didn't want to fail, and I didn't want others to see me as a failure.

I ultimately chose to disregard these thoughts for a fundamental reason: my life is what I make of it. I can only achieve my goals and dreams by giving it my all. I can't do that if I let my doubts and fears hold me back.

 The only way to fly is to try.

Doing something for the first time is both scary and exciting because you can't know exactly what to expect. Obstacles may exist along the way, but finding ways to overcome them becomes part of the fun and the adventure. One of my favorite quotes applies here:

> *"Accept the challenges so that you can feel the exhilaration of victory."*
>
> *– GENERAL GEORGE S. PATTON*

Life is challenging and unpredictable, which is why it can fill us with fear. However, all fears are not created equal. While some fears are legitimate, some fears are imagined, and some fears are unlikely to come true. For instance, as dangerous as it looks, you are unlikely to get hurt or die while whitewater rafting if you go with an experienced guide and follow safety rules. It's the reason many families, even those with children, feel comfortable going on whitewater rafting trips.

In business and in life, experienced guides exist in the form of mentors, coaches, and experts to help you navigate uncharted waters and to help you overcome any doubts, challenges, or fears. If you need them, use them. If you never step outside of your fear and your comfort zone, you will always remain in the exact same place.

Don't let fear stop you. Beyond the fear exists a better life just waiting for you.

A life with more _____.

Go ahead. Fill in that blank for yourself. Is it a life with more success, more love, more health, more wealth, more joy, or more inner peace? You decide.

More is out there waiting for you, and a lack of confidence will no longer hold you back from getting it. Not anymore.

This book will take you on a step-by-step journey to creating inside-out confidence that will move you past your fears to achieve what you want on your own terms.

 By transforming what you think of yourself, you will transform what others think of you.

CONFIDENCE IS SELF-TRUST

The word confidence comes from the Latin word *fidere*, which means "to trust."

Trust is everything. It's the foundation of long-lasting, healthy relationships. Trust between two people creates feelings of safety and connectedness. Trust among team members leads to an increase in communication, collaboration, and execution. With trust, projects move faster and go more smoothly. In contrast, when a relationship lacks trust, it's much harder to be vulnerable and be yourself. You doubt the other person's abilities and assume the worst in them. The same principles apply when talking about self-trust.

Because trust is everything, it's extremely important to develop trust in yourself. Self-trust creates a solid foundation supporting the making of a great life, great relationships, and a great career. Until you establish that safe space of trust in your mind and heart, it will be difficult, and in some instances impossible, for you to do what is necessary to build the life you want.

 Self-confidence in its most basic form is having trust in oneself.

* *Do you trust your abilities?*
* *Do you trust your judgment?*
* *Do you trust yourself to keep the promises you make to yourself?*
* *Do you trust that if you learn and work hard that you will be successful?*
* *Do you trust that you know what is important to you?*
* *Do you trust that you know your purpose?*

When self-trust doesn't exist, fear, worry, and uncertainty fill its place.

Johann Wolfgang von Goethe explained it this way:

"As soon as you trust yourself, you will know how to live."

When you trust yourself, you can enjoy self-acceptance and peace. Peace with who you are, what you want, and the choices you make. You believe in your character, abilities, and strength.

Trust in one's self must be nurtured because trust is the foundation necessary for every relationship, including the relationship you have with yourself.

Confidence without self-trust is hollow. On the outside, people can look and sound confident, but behind closed doors they question their worth and abilities. All it takes is a hurtful comment or a negative experience and their confidence shatters. Compare that with rock-solid confidence that comes from the inside. Its source of strength comes from within, and it's not easily damaged by external words, behaviors, or events.

YOUR BEST SELF

There is a different version of you. It's the person you've always envisioned yourself becoming. This person loves who they are. This person achieves big goals and dreams. This person isn't held back by fear or doubts. This person takes action.

Becoming the best version of yourself isn't about perfection. It's about self-fulfillment. You have a vision of who you can be and what you can accomplish.

What will it take?

It takes self-confidence.

A confident person uses specific thought patterns that propel them toward self-actualization, the fulfillment of one's potential. It begins with the right mindset.

A Confident Person Thinks:

- **Who I am is worthy.**
- **What I want is possible.**
- **Where I go is my decision.**
- **Why I am confident comes from my purpose and values.**

With the right mindset, anything is possible. You can change the world, and you can make a difference.

A confident mindset makes it possible to step outside your comfort zone. You trust that a step forward will result in something better, in something more. More could be landing a dream job, owning a business, adopting a healthier lifestyle, finding love, or running for public office. You have a vision of the joy and success that comes with becoming the best version of yourself, but it takes confidence to pursue that vision.

A Confident Person <u>Takes Action</u>:

- ✓ **Despite the fear.**
- ✓ **Despite the risk.**
- ✓ **Despite what others might think.**
- ✓ **Despite what others are doing.**
- ✓ **Despite never having done it before.**
- ✓ **Despite having failed.**

Taking action leads to many rewards. The people you can help. The experience you will gain. The lessons you will learn. The satisfaction of giving it your best shot.

Action also generates momentum. Once you start, you are much more motivated to continue making progress toward the things you want. Success is the result of many small actions compounding into something big.

The good news is that confidence isn't something you're born with. Confidence is a skill, and the powerful feeling of confidence can be created. Yes, created! Once you learn to create confidence, you will be unstoppable in pursuing your biggest goals and dreams.

THE BENEFITS OF CONFIDENCE

By believing in yourself, others will believe in you, too. It's a powerful combination that will add many positive benefits to your life, such as:

- A mind at peace
- Living life on your own terms
- Motivation to go after what you want
- Making strong decisions
- Willingness to figure things out
- Setting healthy boundaries
- People trusting you
- People listening to what you have to say
- People finding you more attractive
- People viewing you as a leader
- Moving past challenges
- Being happy with yourself

Confidence will also improve your life by removing negative thoughts and feelings such as:

- Anxiety about the future
- Worrying about failure
- Feeling lost or stuck
- Excessive self-doubt
- Hyper self-criticism
- Fear of making mistakes
- Constant comparison to others

 Confidence is the secret to living your best life.

What I love about having confidence is regularly having my mind filled with positive thoughts that give me positive feelings that propel me to take positive action. It makes me feel excited about my present and my future. I also like being the person in my life who has the most influence on my emotional and mental well-being.

What specific benefits do you want to gain from having confidence?

Write them down:

_____

_____

_____

_____

What will you use the power of confidence to gain in your life?

Write them down:

_____

_____

_____

_____

BEING A ROLE MODEL FOR OTHERS

One of my goals as a parent is to raise kind, confident, and independent human beings. If you want confidence for yourself, you most likely want the people you care about to also have confidence because you see the benefits.

Watching others is one of the best ways adults and children learn positive traits and behaviors. When they see you living life in a way that shows you believe in your worth and abilities, they will begin to exhibit confidence in similar ways. Unfortunately, the opposite is also true. If they see you lacking confidence and not pursuing things that are difficult or scary, they will internalize that as well.

Who do you care about who would benefit from you gaining more confidence? Is there someone you want to instill with confidence by being able to model confident behaviors to them?

The people we care about can be our biggest motivators to change and improve. When you better yourself, you often end up bettering the people around you.

FOLLOW THE SYSTEM

Goals give you something to work toward, but you need a system to get you there. If your goal is to have enough confidence to achieve big things in your life, then you need more than willingness and determination to achieve it. You need a system so you can work smarter, not harder.

A system is a specific and predetermined way of doing things consistently. It can be used to change behavior and get reliable results. The best systems use the right combination of simplicity and effectiveness to get the job done. My three-step confidence creation system for achieving unlimited confidence balances simplicity and effectiveness to help individuals transform their lives. Each step builds on the one before it, and the action prompts get you to think and behave in new ways that benefit you long-term. Follow the system. It's a recipe for success.

If you're like me and enjoy cooking, you've probably visited a cooking website to find a new recipe. Many of them allow users to rate the recipe and leave comments. The ratings and comments help other readers determine whether or not the recipe is any good.

A frustration of mine is when people rate a recipe negatively on a website after changing the recipe. For example, I saw a comment online where someone wrote:

> *"This recipe turned out awful. I substituted canola oil for butter, and it didn't turn out right at all. I expected better. One star out of five!"*

A recipe, like a system, must be followed step-by-step to create a consistent end result. Please don't skip a step and wonder why it's not working the way you expected.

Starting something, doing it to the best of your ability, and finishing it all build self-trust. Complete the three-step system in this book from beginning to end, and you will gain unlimited confidence that will change your life.

Diana Rogers Jaeger

STEP #1: CREATE CLARITY

"Your vision will become clear only when you can look into your own heart. Who looks outside, dreams; who looks inside, awakes."

- Carl Jung

Diana Rogers Jaeger

Confidence is an inside job. It comes from knowing yourself.

In the movie *Guardians of the Galaxy* there is an endearing giant tree-like character named Groot. At times calm and peaceful and at other times violently protective of his friends, Groot stands out in a special way in that he only ever says the same three words:

"I am Groot."

No matter the situation or who is talking to him, he always says, "I am Groot." To me, this communicates that he knows who he is and that he wants others to know him. If you think about it, we should all be more like Groot and own who we are.

Confidence is showing up as your authentic self and saying, "I am [YOUR NAME]." There is no need to elaborate. Those three words say it all.

Your journey to confidence begins with getting to know yourself and understanding what makes you, well, YOU!

 Embrace your individuality.

- ☀ Your purpose
- ☀ Your values
- ☀ What makes you happy What
- ☀ makes you strong What
- ☀ motivates you
- ☀ The legacy you want to leave behind

Self-understanding and self-acceptance will make you feel grounded, which means it will be difficult for external sources, such as other people's opinions and judgments, to shake your confidence.

Creating clarity about who you are by knowing what is in your heart and mind is the very first step to developing the type of confidence that comes from within.

SELF-UNDERSTANDING THROUGH
SELF-REFLECTION

Personal transformation requires understanding yourself on a deep level. You can't know what is best for you until you know yourself intimately. For that to happen, you need to intentionally make the time and space for self-reflection—thinking deeply about your thoughts, behaviors, emotions, attitudes, motivations, and desires.

This process of looking inward is similar to looking into a mirror and describing what you see. If you like what you see, you will feel empowered to do more of what you're doing. If you don't like what you see, you will know it's time to make a change.

Throughout this book, you will come across many opportunities for self-reflection. Don't skip them. Skipping the self-reflection activities would be like making big decisions without uncovering all the facts. You will only end up second-guessing yourself or, worse, having regrets. Take your time completing the questions, fill-in-the-blanks, and activities because self-reflection plays a vital role in personal growth and development. When you understand yourself better, you can make better choices and be more intentional with your thoughts and actions.

MAKE YOUR OWN DEFINITIONS

A lack of confidence can occur when a person's self-image does not match the image of who they want to be. For example, a person may desire to be rich, pretty, smart, or successful. However, the definition people have in their minds of what it means to be "pretty" or "successful" are often the definitions given to them by their parents, the media, or society.

Beauty magazines make their profits by telling women how they should look and act like in order to be considered beautiful and desirable by others. There were numerous references to the ideal woman being tall and having thin waists, big breasts, long hair, and full lips. As teenagers and young adults, my friends and I took our definitions of beauty straight out of those glossy pages.

With my height at five feet one inch, no curves, flat chest, frizzy hair, and thin lips, I looked nothing like the women in the pages of those magazines. Since I didn't meet society's beauty standards, I interpreted that to mean I was not a "real" woman. I felt like I had more in common with a teenage boy's body than I did with a woman.

That hurt.

But it hurt the most when I got ridiculed by boys and girls at school for being flat-chested. They teased me because of my breast size, something entirely determined by genetics and out of my control. I hated changing in the locker room because I didn't want anyone to see my A-cups and judge me. I was scared girls would whisper about me behind my back or say something to embarrass me in front of everyone.

My breasts grew bigger in college, and I still felt like they were too small because women in the media flaunted much larger breasts. I continued to feel that way until a monumental event in my life occurred at the age of 30. I became pregnant with my first child. After reading articles about the numerous benefits breastfeeding provides to mother and baby, I committed to breastfeeding my baby until he turned one. But then I questioned, "Are my breasts even big enough to breastfeed?"

After more research on pregnancy and childbirth, I made another big decision. I wanted to have a natural childbirth free of any drugs or interventions. I signed up for Bradley Method birthing classes with my husband, who would serve as my birthing coach. In my 12 weekly classes, I learned things about pregnancy and childbirth that were nothing like what I had seen in TV shows and movies.

Drug-free pain management techniques include moaning and lower back massages. Kneeling and squatting are some of the most effective positions for giving birth. Small breasts do not reduce a person's likelihood of successfully breastfeeding. I learned a great deal about my own body and how the female body is uniquely designed to give birth. As a result, I began to trust and appreciate my body like I never had before.

Unlike the messages shared in the media, my breasts weren't made to be objects of sexual desire. My breasts exist to produce milk with 100% of the nutrients my baby needs for a healthy diet.

My breasts had purpose.

And they served their purpose well! I breastfed both of my sons until the age of one. I went from being unhappy with my breast size to being thankful for my breasts. It didn't matter their size. They were just the right size for my two babies, and they were just the right size for my body. I finally started to appreciate their finer qualities. When running, they didn't bounce painfully. When golfing, they didn't get in the way of my swing. They caused me no back pain. I became happy with my breasts when I started defining their beauty not by their size but by their purpose.

I used to dream of having long, sexy legs like those of models until I started thinking about what my legs do for me. My short legs give me the joy of playing soccer, running, and hiking up mountains. More specifically, my legs made it possible for me to become an All-State soccer player, run fast enough to qualify for the Boston Marathon, and climb 14,000-foot elevation peaks. They allow me to dance with my husband and play with my kids. For me, beautiful legs enable me to be active with my family and participate in my favorite outdoor activities. This definition is 100% mine. It speaks to what is important to me.

Be consciously aware of what you've been programmed to think. The media, especially social media, is full of beauty ideals and standards that are exclusive, unattainable, and unhealthy. Beauty comes in all shapes, colors, and sizes. Beauty is a state of mind.

What are ways to see beauty in the body you were born with? What is your own definition of beauty? How do you define your happiness? What does success mean to you?

Diana Rogers Jaeger

Make your own definitions for what you want in life.

Your definitions need to come from you and no one else. Begin with self-reflection and a blank page.

Having your own definitions that are 100% yours can drastically change your perspective on life and how you see yourself.

The process of defining what is important to you creates core-driven confidence.

Not all confidence is created equally. Winning, beauty, and compliments create short-term confidence that disappears the next time you lose, have a bad hair day, or don't get the positive feedback you expect. Core-driven confidence is steadfast and long-term.

Core-driven confidence gets its strength and power from having a purpose and a clear set of core values.

Since these come from within, they create a self-generated supply of confidence that never runs out. Confidence that depends on compliments and validation from others is unreliable. The supply can get cut off at any time. You may also receive mixed messages where some people like who you are and what you're doing, but others don't approve.

When you know yourself deeply and your actions and decisions align with your purpose and values, what other people think and say won't matter.

Michelle Obama is one of my favorite people and one of the greatest role models for living life with confidence. She spoke about the importance of having your own compass to follow during her commencement address at Tuskegee University.

I have learned that as long as I hold fast to my beliefs and values — and follow my own moral compass — then the only expectations I need to live up to are my own."

– MICHELLE OBAMA

Those who don't know their purpose and core values are likely to live their life according to other people's beliefs and expectations. It goes right back to the trap of pleasing others.

Before I created my own purpose and core values, I was lost, even if I didn't feel like it at the time. Instead of following my own North Star, I wandered from one shiny thing to the next. I kept looking outward for answers when I should have been looking inward.

 The biggest answers you seek are right inside of you.

KNOW YOUR PURPOSE

Kelli Masters is the founder and president of KMM Sports and a National Football League sports agent who overcame sexism to make history. She became the first woman to represent a top-five pick in the NFL draft when her client, Gerald McCoy, signed with the Tampa Bay Buccaneers in 2010.

Masters is only one of a handful of women who are certified NFL agents. It's normal for her to battle against more than 900 male agents for clients. When entering the career field, she knew the odds were stacked against her and that she wouldn't be taken seriously by many people simply because of her sex. She encountered potential clients who didn't want her representing them because she was a woman, even though they believed she was qualified.

Masters recalls a well-respected male NFL agent pointing his finger in her face and saying, "Let me tell you why you don't belong here." He told her, "Players will never respect you. You need to stop wasting your time and do something more appropriate."

These words would have crushed most people and made them instantly doubt themselves. But not Masters. She hit him right back with, "You don't know me. You don't know why I'm here. You don't know what I'm capable of."

His words and opinion didn't matter because Masters knew precisely why she was there.

Her journey to find her purpose began when she decided to start focusing her life on how she could serve others. Before that moment, she admits she was wrapped up in trying to be Ms. Perfect and living her life to impress others and gain their approval.

She found a calling to use her skills and passion to protect athletes and maximize their opportunities. Masters guides them through the NFL draft process, their athletic career, retirement, and even into their second career. In cut-throat negotiations, she fights tooth and nail for her clients because she personally cares about them.

Masters tells the story of how she had a vision when taking the test to become a certified agent. She saw images of young boys playing and knew these boys would need her help one day. However, to help them, she needed to pass the test. Knowing her purpose and why she was taking the test took her from a nervous wreck to someone determined to succeed. She passed that test, even though the majority fail each year.

Years later, when she took several clients to dinner before an upcoming NFL draft, one of them asked her when she became an agent. She did the math and realized the young men with her that evening would have been seven, eight, or nine years old—the exact ages of the boys in her vision.

"Those were my little boys," she said. "That was the reason I took that test."

Knowing her "why" gave Masters the confidence to walk in her purpose and overcome difficult challenges. Sexism wasn't going to stop her from helping people.

"No one can tell me I don't belong," she said.

Because she followed her purpose and did not let the thoughts and opinions of others limit her, Masters has helped many young boys fulfill their dreams of playing in the NFL.

 Your purpose is your motivational why.

It's your joy-filled way of leaving this world better than you found it. It's the reason you get out of bed in the morning. It's why you do what you do.

While I've modified the wording of my purpose over the years, the underlying theme has always been consistent. My purpose, written in the form of a personal mission statement, is this:

"Live a life of adventure while making the world a better place by helping people and organizations become the best version of themselves."

How did I come up with it?

For me, adventure means trying new, exciting things and enjoying the great outdoors. When I am doing these things, I feel happy and fulfilled. Making the world a better place I borrowed from the Girl Scout Mission Statement "Build girls of courage, confidence, and character who make the world a better place." As a dedicated volunteer and Lifetime Member of Girl Scouts and past board president of Girl Scouts Western Oklahoma, I have deeply internalized this mission into my life since my mid-20s when I first became a troop leader and a mentor. It's a big part of my belief system. The last part is how I can use my talents to serve others while making an impact. My purpose gives my life meaning and direction. It is my North Star.

What is your North Star?

If life is a ship, you are its captain, and your purpose will guide you to where you need to go.

 A clear sense of purpose gives you confidence in who you are and what you do.

KNOW YOUR CORE VALUES

Core values are the fundamental beliefs by which a person lives their life. They define the characteristics that are most important to an individual.

 While purpose guides the direction of your life, core values drive your daily decisions and behaviors.

Since every person is unique, each person lives by a different set of core values. One of the easiest ways to see differences in values is with how people choose to spend their money. Some people spend money on gifts because they value expressing their love. Some people spend money on experiences, such as trips or concerts, because they value quality time with others. Some people prioritize saving money for retirement because they value financial freedom.

Jill posts on social media that she bought a new purse. Dylan, a person who likes to spend money on experiences, may consider that materialistic. In contrast, Maria, who likes to save money, might think it's wasteful since Jill already owns a purse.

Dylan talks about his trip to attend his favorite band's concert in New York City. Jill may consider that frivolous since there is nothing tangible to show for that money. However, Maria thinks the money could have been better spent investing in the stock market.

Maria shares how her family follows a strict budget so they can meet their big savings goal for the year. Dylan and Jill may think Maria and her family unnecessarily deprive themselves of nice things and memorable vacations.

They are three individuals with three different value systems. As a result, the choices of one do not match the choices of the others. As long as you spend less than you earn, there is no right or wrong way to spend disposable income. A person should spend it according to their values.

 Your core values go to the heart of who you are and what you believe.

Life is messy and can pull you in a dozen different directions every single day. Millions of messages enter your brain, some contradictory, that tell you to be this or to do that. Who should you listen to? The experts? The media? Family? Friends?

The answer is to listen to *your* values, no matter what anyone else says.

People may judge you for your choices when they are different from their own. Don't let that stop you. What they think about you is none of your business. Living a purpose-driven life according to your core values *is* your business.

My core values influence my actions on regularly. They guide my decisions, big and small, including how I treat others, how I spend my time, and how I spend my money. As a result, I feel confident in my decisions because I am living my life with intention.

My core values are:

Integrity
I believe honesty is the best policy, and I want to be someone people can fully trust.

Appreciation
I am grateful for our beautiful world, my life, and the people in it.

Quality Time
This is my love language, and I feel happiest when I spend time with people I care about.

Collaboration
A team can come up with better solutions than any individual, and it's more fun to work together.

Results-Oriented
I want my life and my work to show real impact.

Win-Win
It's not enough that I win. The world is a better place when we both win.

What are your core values? What are the principles that guide your daily life?

It's important to identify them and to live by them. Together, your purpose and core values are your #1 tool for making confident decisions.

The opposite of fear is clear.

The next time you are faced with multiple options, you can be confident that the right choice is the one that best aligns with your purpose and core values. Your core values will tell you what is important to you and what is not. They will tell you what you will and will not do.

 Your purpose and your core values will always guide you in the right direction.

TIME TO CLIMB ACTIVITIES

The popular saying goes, "Knowledge is power." There is much value in learning and education. However, the greatest power is in applied knowledge—using what you've learned to make an impact. Knowledge is not meant to stay inside your head. By doing nothing with it, your life stays the same. In rock climbing, you may know how to put on the right gear and clip into the rope, but you can't get to the top until you start climbing.

 To change your life, you must apply what you learn. It's time to climb!

Every Time to Climb activity in this book is an opportunity to put your new knowledge into practice. Spend ample time completing each activity before you read the next section. The more you apply what you learn, the faster you develop the mindset and skills that create unlimited confidence.

Many of the activities require you to write down your thoughts and ideas. Select a blank notebook or journal that you will use for all the activities in the book. It's beneficial to have a designated place to capture all of your thoughts and ideas so you can easily refer to them and build on them at later points in time. For example, coming up with your own list of core values may take several attempts as you reflect on what you first wrote down and refine your list. By the time you finish this book, your notebook or journal will be filled with your essence. It will be a valuable tool you can continually use on your confidence journey.

TIME TO CLIMB

Discover your purpose and identify your core values.

Determining your purpose and core values requires self-reflection and answering questions that get to the root of your passions, beliefs, and desires. Find a quiet place to think and listen to your innermost thoughts without interruption.

Imagine yourself at your 80th birthday celebration listening to people take turns talking about your life. Write down your answers to the following questions:

- *What will they remember about you?*
- *What were your main passions in life?*
- *What character traits and values did you consistently demonstrate in your life?*
- *What impact did you have on people?*
- *What accomplishments will they mention?*
- *What was your legacy?*

Think long and deep about the meaning of your answers and what they reveal about what is most important to you.

YOUR PURPOSE

Now that you better understand what is most important to you, what is your purpose in life? What gives your life meaning and direction? What will you do to leave this world better than you found it?

Create a one-sentence personal mission statement that describes your motivational why in life.

There is no single formula for creating a great personal mission statement, although shorter is better because you need to remember it. However, it does have to pass one specific test. You've created a strong personal mission statement when it makes you feel proud to live it, and you're excited to share it with others.

Here are some examples of personal mission statements to inspire you when writing your own:

- *To use my talents to educate women around the world on how to become financially independent.*
- *To be the type of leader that puts people first no matter what.*
- *To instill a lifelong love of learning in small children.*
- *To have fun in my journey through life and learn from my mistakes.*
- *To use my creative potential to create entertaining stories that make people feel powerful emotions.*
- *To inspire others to protect wildlife and the environment for our children's future.*
- *To know even one life has breathed easier because I have lived.*

My purpose in life is to:

_____

_____

_____

_____

_____

_____

_____

YOUR CORE VALUES

What values or principles guide your personal code of conduct?

What qualities or characteristics are essential to who you are?

What must you have in your life to experience fulfillment?

Write down the values that came up in your answers on individual sticky notes. Group similar ones together. Take time to reflect on your answers, and then prioritize them in order of importance.

Narrow your core values to your Top 5. Having too many will make it difficult to remember them all, and too few won't be enough to adequately guide your decision-making.

YOUR TOP 5 CORE VALUES

1.

2.

3.

4.

5.

Write a sentence next to each one that describes why it's important to you.

When going through this process, be extra careful to make sure the purpose and values you write down are truly yours and not someone else's. The belief system of the people in your life, whether it's a spouse, parent, or friend, may not be in harmony with what is important to you. In addition, your core values should reflect who you are now and not who you aspire to be. No one should be surprised by your core values. I encourage you to share your list of core values with people you trust who will give you honest feedback.

Lastly, your purpose and core values are not set in stone. It's normal for them to evolve over time. As you grow and life experiences teach you more about yourself and what truly matters to you, adjust them as needed.

CHOOSE YOUR OWN PATH TO SUCCESS

Society, teachers, and parents ingrain children with the belief that to be successful they need to (A) earn a high school diploma, (B) earn a college degree, and (C) get a good job with good benefits.

Schools do a good job of teaching kids the ABCs and the A-B-C steps to success. I grew up believing this definition of success without questioning it. After all, it made sense, and I assumed that adults knew what was best for me. I followed the path that had been laid out before me.

I graduated high school, and when I graduated with my degree from the University of Oklahoma, I started looking for a good job with good benefits. I found myself working for a government agency that paid 100% of my healthcare and gave me three weeks of paid vacation in addition to paid federal and state holidays. I did it! I had followed the A-B-C steps to success.

Then as a young professional, I defined the next stage of success as earning more money and working my way up the career ladder to an executive position. With more money, I could buy a bigger house and a nicer car. It was the path to what everyone referred to as the American Dream—a true sign of success.

One day at work, my mentor suggested I read his copy of *The Four-Hour Work Week* by Timothy Ferriss. In his book, Ferriss talks about two concepts that shattered my view of the American Dream. He talked about the concepts of "lifestyle design" and "mini-retirements." These concepts bucked the norm and societal pre-conditioning and presented new opportunities.

Lifestyle design is about intentionally setting up your life to allow you to live and work on your own terms.

I saw a different life for myself. My ideal lifestyle involved plenty of time to spend with my family and go on outdoor adventures. Some of my favorite activities are tent camping and hiking, which require more time than money.

When I traveled to Spain on my honeymoon, I met ordinary citizens on their two- or three-month "holiday." Holiday is what many other English-speaking countries call a vacation. How was it possible they had that much time off work?

I later learned that other countries enjoy 16 to 30 paid vacation days each year. While my husband and I were busy cramming as many places and activities as possible into our two-week honeymoon, the people we met on holiday had the time to leisurely spend a week or more in the same area. They could immerse themselves in a place and its culture instead of doing the American drive-by style of traveling.

A mini-retirement is a set period of time taken off from working to purposefully enjoy life to its fullest now instead of waiting until traditional retirement when a person's much older and not in as great of health.

The retirement age in America is 62 years old. I enjoy going on backpacking trips in the wilderness. I can say with confidence 62-year old Diana will not enjoy carrying a

30-pound pack up a mountain and sleeping on the ground as much as I do now. She will want her memory foam mattress and somewhere to plug in her margarita machine.

The typical American Dream requires working 40+ hours a week, five days a week, with only two to four weeks of vacation each year. That is not the lifestyle I wanted, and it doesn't allow for mini retirements. I knew it would be highly unlikely I could go on extended periods of vacation working for someone else. I needed to work for myself and have the freedom to create my own schedule. The idea planted itself in my brain. Years later, I would act on that idea.

Being called "The American Dream" implies that it should be every American's dream.

By identifying what was most important to me, it was clear that American Dream was not my dream at all. The American Dream placed greater value on money than time, and I valued time more than money.

Ferriss opened my eyes to the possibilities and rewards of lifestyle design. I realized I had been blindly following societal norms of happiness and success instead of creating my own definitions of happiness and success and making life choices that directly supported them.

It was clear the A-B-C plan was no longer for me. I picked the Be-Me plan—a life designed by me and aligned with my purpose and values.

I share this story because your purpose and values may or may not match what is popular or mainstream. You don't need anyone's approval to live your life the way you want it, and don't let what other people might think change your mind. You know who you are and what is important to you, and they don't.

When you find yourself wavering and having doubts in life, remember these words of wisdom:

> *"Success is liking yourself, liking what you do,*
> *and liking how you do it."*

> *– MAYA ANGELOU*

 With confidence, you can live a life that is true to yourself and not the life others expect of you.

DEVELOP A VISION OF YOUR FUTURE

Greatness starts in your mind.

In his highly influential book *The Seven Habits of Highly Effective People*, Stephen Covey discusses the importance of beginning with the end in mind. He states that all things are created twice, first a mental creation and then a physical creation. In other words, people can only be intentional with their actions when they have a vision of where they want to go.

Life is too short to let the winds of chance and circumstances blow you around. Your future is in your hands, and it starts with a clear understanding of your desired destination. Your vision should be so compelling that it excites and motivates you to work towards it daily.

The most motivated people know exactly what they are trying to achieve. Their mind creates a high-definition picture of what their desired future looks like. Because they can see it, they strongly believe in it. Their vision is so clear that they can feel what success feels like before it's achieved.

 Visualization is a powerful way to practice success.

 **TIME TO CLIMB**

*Develop a clear vision of something specific
you want to achieve.*

Describe in specific detail the following and write it down:

* ☀ What do you want to achieve?
* ☀ What are the reasons you want to achieve it?
* ☀ Use all five senses. What does success look, feel, hear, taste, and smell like?
* ☀ How does your goal relate to your values, purpose, or personal mission statement?

Once you've developed a clear vision, the next step is to turn it into a physical vision board. A vision board is a collection of photos and images that represents your vision and inspires you to achieve that vision. Once you've created your vision board, put it where you view it every day. By seeing your vision in great detail, you are more likely to take steps to achieve it.

KNOW WHAT MAKES YOU FEEL LOVED AND APPRECIATED

I used to think men were from Mars and women were from Venus. It explained why the two sexes have communication breakdowns where we can't understand each other.

There was a period of time when my husband, Kevin, and I were dating that we lived on opposite sides of a large metropolitan city. As a result of the driving distance, we didn't see each other as often as I would have liked. It upset me when he wouldn't come over to my house when he didn't have other plans. It seemed like he would rather do nothing than hang out with me. I felt hurt and frustrated that he didn't understand why spending time together was important to me.

Then I came across a book that changed my worldview about what makes people feel loved and what makes relationships strong. It's called *The 5 Love Languages* by Dr. Gary Chapman. It taught me that people receive and express love in five universal ways.

The 5 Love Languages are:

1. Words of Affirmation
2. Quality Time
3. Acts of Service
4. Receiving Gifts
5. Physical Touch

A person's love language is Words of Affirmation if kind words, compliments, and love notes are highly important to them. Individuals who love Quality Time want your undivided attention and to do things together. Those who value Acts of Service feel loved when you help them and do nice things for them. Others experience love and affection from Receiving Gifts. They value the gift itself and the thoughtfulness that went into choosing and getting the gift. Lastly, some individuals value Physical Touch the most out of the 5 Love Languages. They crave physical affection from their partner, such as hugs, caresses, or massages.

When two people in a relationship speak different love languages and don't communicate their love in a way that is meaningful to the other person, it leads to negative emotions.

You will feel hurt and unloved if your love language is not spoken to you.

After taking the 5 Love Languages Quiz, I learned that the love language most important to me is Quality Time. No wonder I got easily upset when my boyfriend turned down an opportunity to spend an evening with me! It finally made sense! Spending time with the people I love is extremely important to me. Kevin's love language is Acts of Service. He showed me he loved me by doing things for me, but that wasn't my love language.

When it comes to feeling loved, differences have nothing to do with being male or female. It depends on your love language. It's essential to speak someone's love language and for them to speak yours if you want to be in fulfilling, long-lasting relationships.

I highly recommend reading *The 5 Love Languages* and taking the free Love Language Quiz online. The knowledge you gain will increase your self-understanding and improve the quality of your personal and romantic relationships.

Encourage the people you care about to take the Love Language Quiz as well, and discuss your love languages with each other. By understanding one another's love language, you can help ensure your love tank is full and the love tanks of the most important people in your life.

Similarly, it's important to know what makes you feel appreciated. The book *The 5 Languages of Appreciation in the Workplace*, which is based on the 5 Love Languages, will help you understand which language makes you feel that you are valued and you matter.

 Greater self-understanding leads to greater self-confidence.

You must understand your emotional needs in your personal and professional relationships. The better you know yourself, the more confidence you will have in communicating your needs and ensuring they are met.

KNOW YOUR STRENGTHS

As human beings, we all have our strengths and weaknesses. While we all have shortcomings that can and should be improved, we have an increased chance of happiness and success when we focus on our strengths.

Understanding your strengths allows you to tap into your talents and pinpoint where you create the most value.

In sixth grade, I took a personality test called True Colors that helped me recognize my natural "Gold" tendencies related to planning, organization, and being detail-oriented.

I learned that I am focused on achieving goals and that I am more rational than emotional. It helped me understand myself better and the people around me who have different natural tendencies in the way they think and communicate because they are either Blue, Orange, or Green.

As a young professional, I learned from an assessment I took in the book *StrengthsFinder 2.0* that my strengths include having high standards, a strong work ethic, and a desire to continuously learn and improve. As a result of having that self-understanding, when I'm part of a team or a project, I am confident in what I bring to the table.

I've also found value in taking the DiSC Profile assessment, which identifies communication styles, and the Enneagram Personality Test, which uncovers an individual's deepest desires and motivations.

There are many different strengths and personality profiles available that can help you better understand yourself. Take one or two of them to help you clarify what makes you different and special. Find out what unique qualities you bring you the table.

This kind of self-awareness is a huge step in building confidence and becoming comfortable in your own skin. It's easier to show up and face the world when you understand why you think and behave the way you do. You feel empowered to show up as your unique self because you know how you positively impact others with your combination of strengths and personality traits.

At the same time, you've gained the self-awareness to know when you need to adapt your communication style when working with people who are different and when it's a good idea to lean on the strengths of others.

 Making the time and effort for self-discovery allows you to know yourself best. That level of clarity creates confidence.

REVEAL YOURSELF

Journaling is an emotional expression of your life. Think of it as painting your life in words. It's one of the best ways to get to know yourself on a deep level.

What you write about and how you express yourself in words can reveal a lot about you.

Whether it's your thoughts, your mood, feelings, inner desires, worries, or day-to-day experiences, it feels good to get them out of your head and put them on paper. Seeing them in writing allows you to view them from a different perspective and to understand them more clearly.

It is said that writing bridges the conscious and the unconscious mind. When that happens, you get a lot of aha moments. Understanding your thought process and finding clarity and insights are huge benefits of journaling. They're why journaling is such a transformative and cathartic experience for many people.

"I write because I don't know what I think until I read what I say."

– FLANNERY O'CONNOR

As you journal, you learn about yourself as you write, and you learn about yourself when you read what you've written. It's a simultaneous act of talking and listening to yourself.

Journaling is widely known to be therapeutic. It gives people time and space to process and make sense of their thoughts and feelings. For instance, journaling is a healthy way to manage stress. When something is bothering you, don't keep it locked up inside. Write about it. It feels good to vent, and articulating your problems into words will give you a lot of insight. Journaling is also a quick and effective way to boost your mood. When you write about the good things in your life, you will immediately feel happier and more grateful.

Journaling is a ritual worth your time, even if it's five minutes a day or 15 minutes a week. Oprah Winfrey, Warren Buffet, Lady Gaga, and Tim Ferriss have all been known to journal extensively. I've been journaling since grade school, and I have no plans of stopping because the experience brings me joy. When I journal, I feel like I'm talking to a trusted friend. It's also part of my self-care because it helps me self-regulate my mental and emotional health.

When it comes to journaling, there is no right or wrong way to do it. All you need is a blank page, either in paper or digital form, and you can write about any topic that opens you up to self-reflection and emotional expression. You may choose to write in complete sentences or create bulleted lists to express your thoughts. You could use a journaling app that is searchable and sends you reminders.

The most important thing is to journal consistently for maximum benefits.

 The more you know yourself, the easier it is to live your life with intention.

 TIME TO CLIMB

Start a journal or diary and have intimate conversations with yourself.

Here are some journal prompts to get you started. Pick three and write down your answers. Next week, pick three more to journal about.

1. What is unique about you?
2. What do you value about yourself?
3. What is something new or exciting in your life?
4. What is something good that you made happen?
5. What are five things for which you are grateful?
6. What happened recently that you always want to remember?
7. What brings you joy?
8. What makes you feel calm and peaceful?
9. What makes you feel powerful?
10. What are your top priorities in life?
11. Who are the people in your life who make you feel safe and why?
12. What do you want to be different in your life one year from now and why?

13. What would you do if you weren't afraid to fail?
14. What is a challenge you have overcome?
15. What is a favorite childhood memory?
16. What is your favorite quote and why?
17. What is your dream life and why?
18. What is something you are willing to work hard for?
19. What do you want more of in your life?
20. What do you want less of in your life?

Key Points of Step #1: Create Clarity

- Have a clear purpose and set of core values
- Create your own definition of success
- Know your strengths and love language

STEP #2: CREATE SELF-TRUST

"Self-trust is the first secret of success."

- Ralph Waldo Emerson

Now that you have clarity by knowing what is important to you, it's time to begin a habit of trusting yourself. Trust is the glue that binds all relationships. This is especially true when it comes to the relationship you have with yourself. Without self-trust, it's hard to believe in yourself, and it's easy to question your worth and abilities.

A big reason why many people can't maintain a high level of self-trust is because they are always looking for approval and acceptance from others. It's an endless cycle and self-defeating because the standards for approval and acceptance differ from person to person. What pleases your parents isn't going to please your friends.

When you're always trying to please everyone, you can never trust that what you're doing is the right thing, especially if it's different from what everyone else is doing.

You'll constantly doubt yourself.

"What if people don't like the way I look?"

"What if my friends don't approve of who I'm dating?"

"What if my parents disagree with my choices?"

That is why it's better to look internally than externally for guidance on what you should do. If it aligns with your values and purpose or makes you truly happy, then it doesn't matter what everyone else thinks. By staying true to who you are and what is important to you, you set yourself free from needing external validation.

Trust that by knowing yourself best, you know what is best for you.

This section of the book will help you develop your self-trust layer by layer. As you train your mind to think differently about yourself, you will create core-driven confidence that stays with you.

ACCEPT THAT YOU LIKE WHAT YOU LIKE

Someone's tastes are the things they personally like, such as their taste in food, clothing, or music. A person's tastes are usually not based on logic but on what brings them joy. That means there are no right or wrong answers. What is considered "good" taste this year could be considered "bad" taste next year.

Popular opinion constantly changes. You shouldn't let it change who you are. Being confident means accepting your tastes or preferences, even if they are different or unpopular.

When it comes to accepting your tastes, use this power phrase:

"I like what I like."

The next time someone questions your taste and asks you in a judging tone, "You're going to wear *that*?" or "*That's* what you like?", don't defend your taste or apologize. Confidently tell them, "I like what I like."

If you like something, it obviously brings you joy. That's a good thing! The world would be a happier place if we allowed ourselves and others to like what we like without judgment. No matter what you do, not everyone is going to agree. Not even everyone can agree with liking chocolate!

Self-confidence is trusting yourself. Whenever you question your taste and your choices because of what people might think or say, you're essentially telling yourself, "I don't trust myself to know what brings me joy."

The idea that another person knows better than you what makes you happy is absurd. You know exactly what brings you joy. Listen to your own opinion.

 Knowing yourself and accepting yourself is a source of confidence every person can tap into.

 **TIME TO CLIMB**

Appreciate your good taste.

You can be confident in accepting your tastes when you reflect on what about them makes you happy. Write down your "I Like What I Like" list using the examples below to get you started.

My "I Like What I Like" List

What about my taste brings me joy:

Example: Folk music

I grew up listening to it with my biological father and adoptive father, and it brings back happy childhood memories.

Example: Pixie hairstyle

It takes less time to fix, and it doesn't blow in my face.

_____

_____

_____

KEEP PROMISES TO YOURSELF

A promise is a promise. It's not something you only do if you're in the right mood or if it's easy or convenient. Since confidence is trusting yourself, self-integrity and the ability to keep promises to yourself are absolutely essential.

I have known people who regularly keep promises to others but regularly break promises to themselves. They won't let others down, but they consistently let themselves down. They promise themselves they will lose weight, get a degree, or become better organized, but they don't do it. There is a lack of follow-through. In plain and simple terms, they've lied to themselves. No one likes liars because they can't be trusted. That is not the type of relationship you want to have with yourself.

 You want to be the person you can trust more than anyone else in the world.

Since you are 100% in control of your actions, this is 100% achievable. It starts by keeping promises to yourself. Stop making excuses and do everything in your power to keep your commitments. Show yourself again and again that you can count on yourself to follow through.

Confidence is self-trust. You build self-trust when you can rely on yourself to turn your words into actions.

When you trust yourself, you become unstoppable. You feel confident in trying new things and taking on new challenges.

With every promise you keep, you also affirm to yourself that you are worth it. The discipline, the extra effort, the sacrifice—it's all worth doing for you to have the life you want. You are important, and you are deserving.

You must create a consistent track record of keeping promises to yourself. How do you start that track record?

 Only make promises to yourself that you expect yourself to keep.

Expecting to keep a promise has more weight than simply wanting to keep a promise. Expecting is a strong belief that something _is_ going to happen. You're serious about it.

What is something you expect yourself to do or achieve?

One thing that has led me to live a consistently healthy lifestyle is that I expect myself to be fit enough to take my children and future grandchildren on many outdoor adventures. I want that quality time with them.

Start with small promises and work your way up to bigger ones. A promise kept is a promise kept no matter how small. Start with losing one pound this month or organizing one closet. Get it done, and enjoy how good it feels to do what you told yourself you would do. It's a feeling you will want to repeat over and over again. Soon, you will have a history of behaving and feeling trustworthy that leads to increased self-confidence.

Write down your track record of trust building. It's great to know something, but it's even more effective when you can see it for yourself. In a journal, write down all of the small, medium, and big promises that you make to yourself and keep. Seeing it in black and white will help you recognize the trust you are building with yourself.

It's a powerful feeling when you can say,

"I trust myself."

REMEMBER YOUR HISTORY OF DOING HARD THINGS

Lack of confidence can come from not trusting in your abilities. You don't believe you can do something successfully because you've never done it before or it's challenging.

The thought, "I'll never be able to do that," pops into your head. However, it's a belief that doesn't hold weight if you remember that you have a history of doing hard things. You have faced a challenge before, and you didn't quit. You have tried something new even though you were scared.

I remember my very first concert band performance in 7th grade. I gripped my alto saxophone tightly as I stepped under the bright lights of the school stage with my fellow band members. So many people were staring at us, waiting for the concert to begin. My forehead and fingers started to sweat. As we started playing the first song, I prayed my instrument wouldn't squeak loudly and cause me to embarrass myself in front of everyone.

It was a huge relief to put that first performance behind me because I felt nervous the entire time. The first time is usually the hardest, and I got through it. I had been there, done that.

I performed in my second concert and then my third and fourth. With every experience, I started getting used to the bright lights and the audience staring. I never again felt as nervous as I did in that first performance, not even in 8th grade when I performed my first solo in the school jazz band.

I survived a hard thing in 7th grade. I know you've survived hard things too, as a child and as an adult. You survived your first day in a brand-new school or a brand-new job. Perhaps you completed the nerve-racking driving test required to obtain your driver's license.

With each experience, you became a little stronger and a little more resilient. You realize that things get easier the more you do them. Your fear of the unknown subsides.

As you focus on building confidence to tackle a new challenge in the present, it's important to remember the many hard things you've done in the past. It doesn't matter if it "should" have been easy because it was easy for someone else. If it was hard for you and you got through it, count it as a win.

Your experiences of doing hard, uncomfortable things give you earned confidence. It's earned because you put in the effort to obtain it. Since you've already done hard things in the past, you've earned the confidence to know you can handle a new challenge. Your track record of doing hard things throughout your life prepared you.

For example, if you overcame a speech impediment, you can then take that earned confidence into your next sales pitch. Training yourself to speak differently is much harder than hearing someone say, "No."

 Think to yourself, "If I did that, I can do this!"

This mindset helped me overcome my fear of public speaking. In my high school English class, I thought to myself, "If I can get on stage in front of hundreds of people to play my saxophone, I can give an oral book report in front of my class." I trusted myself to overcome my nervousness and do a good job because I had done it before in concert band. My earned confidence allowed me to believe I could successfully rise to a new challenge.

 Doing something that scares you builds confidence.

You will start to trust yourself more and more in new situations. No matter the outcome, you are a winner just for trying because you will grow and learn from the experience.

Take a walk down memory lane and think of the hard things you've done or lived through. Grab hold of the positive feelings that surface and let them fuel you to take on your next challenge. Believe you will not only survive it as you've done many times before but there is a good chance you will succeed.

 TIME TO CLIMB

Make a list of the hardest things you've done.

Reflecting on the hard things you've done makes you mentally strong and resilient. List five of the hardest things you are proud of doing, regardless of their outcome. Then, write down all of the reasons why you are proud you did them.

5 Hard Things You've Done and Why You're Proud You Did Them

1.

2.

3.

4.

5.

FOCUS ON THOUGHTS THAT FUEL YOU

When people want to accomplish something, they feel excited and full of anticipation. They are hopeful that it will turn out well. They see themselves asking for the raise or promotion they deserve. They see themselves learning a new hobby, such as surfing or snowboarding. They see themselves going back to school to start a new career that will improve their life.

They are exhilarated by the possibility of getting what they want—more money, more happiness, more opportunity, and more confidence. They focus on the rewards.

But what often happens next derails people from their vision of a better future. They begin to focus exclusively on the risks. Their mind jumps to the worst-case scenario— failure. They think, "If I fail, people will think I'm a loser. I'll be humiliated. It's not worth it." If they've tried before to get what they want and didn't succeed, they think, "I've tried once already, and I failed. This time won't be any different. There's no point in trying again."

It only takes a few seconds for your thoughts to kill your dreams and your confidence. But only if you let them.

People's inner thoughts fall into two types of buckets.

 Your thoughts can either rule you or they can fuel you.

Your thoughts rule you when you let them repress and control you. Like an oppressive dictator, they limit your free will to think and act. Listening to negative thoughts diminishes your confidence and keeps you prisoner of self-limiting beliefs such as:

"If I try, I will fail and everyone will laugh at me."

On the flip side, your thoughts fuel you when they fill you with excitement and motivation to take steps toward your goal. They empower you to overcome any obstacles in your path. These types of thoughts build on one another to develop a positive mindset that believes:

"I can never be a failure if I try and give it my best shot."

The same thought can either rule you or fuel you, depending on your perspective. For instance, a person sets a goal of running a marathon in under 4 hours. The thought of having a faster-than-average finish time could make someone want to train harder. It fuels them. On the other hand, the thought of having a faster than average finish time could lead someone to worrying about maintaining such a fast pace that they decide they don't want to run a marathon anymore. Thoughts of failure rule their mind before they even started.

 Whether your thoughts rule you or they fuel you is your choice.

While you can't always choose what thoughts pop into your head, you always have a choice on where you focus your attention and energy. You have the ability to weed out the thoughts that plant seeds of doubt about your worth and capabilities. Take the time to feed the thoughts that grow and strengthen your self-confidence.

It's time to put a stop to thoughts in your mind that make you want to stop or quit.

What happens if I fail?

What happens if I'm told "No"?

What happens if I'm not good enough?

What happens if I don't succeed?

When negative thoughts creep inside your head that make you question yourself, you must be prepared to do something about them. It's not enough to ignore them. You must replace them with positive thoughts and actions.

Here are three helpful strategies to defeat negative thoughts:

1. **Stop replaying them in your mind.**
   What you pay attention to grows bigger. Don't feed the negativity by letting it constantly live in your mind.

2. **Create strong, positive comebacks.**
   The best way to stop replaying negative thoughts in your mind is to drown them out with louder positive thoughts. If your thoughts tell you that you suck, tell yourself 10 good reasons why you know you don't suck. If you are convinced you won't succeed, tell yourself the benefits of showing up and at least trying. Here are some examples:

   "Even if things don't turn out exactly like I want, I will have learned something I can use going forward."

   "By trying, I am one step closer to my goal."

   "I have people in my life I can go to for help if I need it."

3. **Prove your positive thoughts right.**
Build more self-trust by doing things that confirm your positive thoughts. Actions are always more convincing than words. Creating alignment between the thoughts that fuel you and your behavior is the fastest way to defeat self-doubt.

Practice these strategies so you can effectively combat negative self-talk anytime it occurs. Before long, you will have trained your mind to habitually focus on the thoughts that fuel you.

Valerie Riley is the owner of LifeSquire, a company that provides personal assistant services to busy business owners. She started her company in her 20s and has grown it immensely, but not without setbacks.

When the hard work she put into franchising LifeSquire didn't grow her business as planned, Valerie used a personal mantra to overcome her thoughts and feelings of failure. She told herself over and over again,

"Everything is working out for my highest good."

Valerie believes that even negative events will ultimately lead to positive outcomes if she keeps moving toward her vision. Instead of mentally torturing herself about what went wrong, she pivoted and started looking for a different path to success.

When Valerie feels stressed from the many demands of running a business, she focuses her energy on what she can accomplish in the next 24 hours. She tells herself, "All you can do is what you can do in a day." This mindset keeps her from feeling overwhelmed and reminds her that even small progress is progress.

Valerie exemplifies a person who has learned to generate positive thoughts that fuel her forward.

GIVE YOURSELF A SELF-TALK PEP TALK

It's normal to experience fear and self-doubt. Even people who consider themselves confident are not immune from having them. Why? It's because of the existence of negativity bias. Human beings instinctively pay more attention to negative information, events, and emotions than their positive counterparts.

If you make a mistake or someone criticizes you, you may have a hard time not thinking about it. You may start judging yourself harshly, dwelling on your weaknesses, and creating negative self-talk. If that happens, it's what you think and do next that make all the difference.

Do you keep listening to the trash-talk on NEGATIVE FM, or do you switch channels to the uplifting messages on POSITIVE FM?

While you might not be able to completely turn off the negative self-talk, you can do something to turn its volume down to a whisper.

 Confident people know how to give themselves a self-talk pep talk.

For every single negative thought that enters your mind, it's necessary to counteract it with at least three positive thoughts.

When I experienced writer's block, the thought, "What if I can't finish my book this year?" crept into my mind repeatedly. It always came with a sick feeling in my stomach because I didn't want to let myself or others down. I needed to stop the negative self-talk right away before it damaged my confidence.

I started giving myself self-talk pep talks by telling myself self-affirming facts as to why I would finish this book. Here are some of the ones I used:

1. I have a long track record of meeting deadlines and finishing projects.

2. This book is deeply important to me, and I will use it to help others.

3. I have a book coach who I meet with every week to hold me accountable and help me finish it.

These reasons reminded me that I am a hard-working person who does what I say I will do. I went a step further by writing down my self-talk pep talks in my journal. My doubts disappeared, and I began to believe in myself again. I started thinking, "I am definitely finishing this book this year." My self-affirming thoughts strengthened my self-trust and fueled my motivation to keep writing.

Words are powerful. If the words you tell yourself don't build you up, it's time to edit them. Your positive self-talk must always outweigh your negative self-talk.

 What you tell yourself changes who you become.

Think positive thoughts, and write them down. Putting them on paper gives your positive thoughts more power than the negative ones in your head. They are no longer abstract. You can see them, read them, and touch them. They become self-affirming truths on which you base your actions.

Self-talk pep talks are stronger when they relate to your purpose, your values, and factors that you control, such as your attitude and effort. It also helps to cite examples from your past or present that prove your negative thoughts are invalid.

Negative thoughts come too easily and stay too long, so it's important to develop the mental habit of quickly shutting them down. With three positive thoughts, you can completely change the conversation in your mind.

 When you think differently, you feel differently.
When you feel differently, you act differently.

 **TIME TO CLIMB**

Create a self-talk pep talk.

What is a self-limiting thought or belief that recently popped into your head?

Write down three positive reasons why that belief is inaccurate or false.

1.

2.

3.

Tell yourself these three things over and over until you erase the self-limiting thought or belief from your mind.

TRUST YOURSELF TO FIND THE ANSWERS

Did you know that when Elon Musk started pursuing his vision of developing self-driving cars, he didn't have an exact plan for how to build one? When Jeff Bezos started selling books on Amazon, he didn't know it would later become one of the world's most innovative technology companies. Sara Blakely, the world's youngest self-made billionaire, knew nothing about clothing manufacturing when she had the idea to make footless pantyhose. She started her company, Spanx, anyway.

These individuals didn't have all the answers, but they all had a vision.

A vision is a clear mental picture of what you want to do or create. In it, you can see your preferred future.

Think about your vision for the life or the career that you want to achieve. You may not have all the answers right now for how to make it happen. That is okay. Don't let that stop you.

Many people never act on their vision because they don't believe they have enough knowledge, skills, or experience to take the first step. However, when you have a vision, you already possess the one thing you need to get started because you can see where you want to go.

 It is through starting that you find the answers, and the answers start to find you.

When I started writing this book, I didn't know a lot about the book-writing process. However, I had a clear vision of changing people's lives by sharing my journey and the mindset and behaviors that create confidence.

My vision would never have come true if I had never started. The universe was telling me the same thing when I came across the following statement on the Internet:

> *"You can have your book or you can have your excuses, but you can't have both."*

Excuses are reasons used to avoid doing something or to justify why something has or hasn't been done. Saying you can't do something because you don't have enough information is making an excuse. We live in the Information Age, which means many answers are only a few clicks away. Get the answers you need!

 Excuses get you nowhere. Action takes you one step closer to your vision.

Beginning is half the battle, so I took action. I created a book outline. I started looking for a book writing coach who could guide me and provide the answers I needed. I emailed a friend who was a published author to ask for referrals, and I contacted book- writing coaches I found from my online research. I picked the best one that met my needs and hired her. I also started scheduling interviews with friends and colleagues to learn about their confidence journey and to gain a broader perspective for my book. I scheduled blocks of time in my calendar to write, and I wrote.

I took all of these action steps within one month, and I immediately went from wanting to write a book to writing a book!

Once I started writing, I found inspiration everywhere. I would read an article, have a conversation, or make an observation that made me want to keep writing. If I hadn't already started writing about confidence, I most likely would have read the same article or had the same conversation but not experienced them or thought about them in the same way. Pretty soon, I was making significant progress toward my vision and adding new sections to my book not in my original outline. As I said, once you start, the answers start finding you.

Like Musk, Bezos, and Blakely, you don't need to know all of the details or answers upfront in order to be successful. Too many people get hung up on the details. Get started on your vision and believe that by taking the first step, you will figure out what you need to do to take the second step, the third step, and so on.

Fear of not having all of the answers can stem from a person's experiences in school. Students are taught the correct answers, and teachers expect them to give the right answers when called on in class. Academic tests grade students on how many right answers they know. Those who don't know enough answers automatically fail the test. These experiences naturally pre-condition many people to believe that they will fail by not having all of the answers, so they don't even try.

 Often, there is more value in the learning process than there is in having the right answers.

Think about a scientist doing an experiment. They are excited to ask a new question, conduct research, make an educated guess, and test their prediction. With every experiment, they learn something useful. Being a scientist isn't about knowing all the answers. It's about asking a lot of questions. A willingness to learn, try, and seek out the answers is a major factor in a person's likeliness to succeed.

 Confidence is trusting in your ability to figure things out as you go.

In fact, "I will find out the answer" is one of the most powerful sentences in the English language.

The pace of change and the amount of data that exists in the world continues to increase. Today's answer may be outdated next week. In the real world, knowing how to find the answer is far more valuable than knowing the answer. It means a person is both resourceful and a problem-solver.

The Internet and libraries are filled with millions of resources for learning and obtaining information. Books, articles, and videos give people access to new knowledge and skills. Librarians help people research and find the information they need, and they provide their services for free. If the library doesn't have the information you need, librarians will refer you to other organizations or resources in the community.

We grow up thinking that learning happens in a school setting, but the majority of learning comes from real-life experiences. For example, you can only learn so much from reading a cookbook or watching a cooking show. The best way to learn how to cook is to get in a kitchen and practice cooking!

Experiential learning is the process of acquiring knowledge, skill, and meaning from direct experience. The experiential learning cycle goes: Experience – Reflect – Think – Act. It begins with having a direct experience, such as hands-on learning. By reflecting on that experience, people develop ideas about the world. People then try out those ideas to see if they are accurate, which leads to a new experience, and the cycle begins all over again.

One of my favorite methods of experiential learning is to interview someone about what they do, sometimes referred to as informational interviews. I remember meeting an executive coach early in my professional career. At the time, I had heard of executive coaches but never met one in real life. Her career intrigued me, and I asked her if we could meet sometime so I could learn more about her profession. She invited me to her office the following week, and with my pen and notepad in hand, I asked her all of my burning questions.

* *What made you want to become an executive coach?*
* *How does the coaching process work?*
* *What types of people do you work with?*
* *What do you enjoy best about coaching?*

She was very open and friendly, and we had a wonderful conversation. Like most people, she was happy to talk about her work with someone genuinely interested. I learned a lot about the coaching process from that experience, and it was more meaningful than simply reading about executive coaching. It's interesting to note that more than a decade after that meeting, I became an executive coach myself.

There are many ways to learn and get the answers you need. Other types of direct experiences are trying something new, trial and error, group discussions, job shadowing, internships, and volunteering.

The next time you feel stuck or feel scared to move forward with your idea or your vision because you don't have all of the answers, remember this: The most successful people you know didn't have everything figured out right from the start.

You don't need the perfect plan to get started.

Begin your journey anyway and take that first step towards your vision. Trust yourself to find the answers and to learn what you need to know.

DON'T BE AFRAID OF BEING TOLD "NO"

Fear or rejection starts early in life. During elementary school, there is the fear of not making any friends, getting picked last on a team, and being made fun of for being different. In middle school and high school, the fear of romantic rejection can feel all-consuming. Even as adults, the painful thought of getting rejected prevents people from applying for a job or asking someone out. For females, the social stigma of making the first move can add another layer of fear—being rejected by society for not acting like a "proper" lady.

My junior year in high school, I worked as a cashier at a grocery store in my hometown. I find it ironic that self-checkout lines have turned me into a cashier again, but now I don't get paid to do it. My co-worker was a really cute sophomore, and I developed a massive crush on him. To protect the innocent, let's call him Colton. Anytime I pulled into the parking lot and saw Colton's pick-up truck, I felt tingly with excitement.

When I was feeling especially brave, I would initiate a conversation with him despite the butterflies in my stomach I always felt when he was around. My secret crush went on for months, and he had no idea how I felt about him. I had no real plans to let him know, but then prom season arrived. The question on everyone's lips at school was, "Who are you taking to prom?"

Without a doubt, I wanted Colton to be my prom date. I knew he would treat me well and look extra handsome in a tuxedo. I imagined us having a great time and eventually becoming boyfriend and girlfriend. In my vision, asking Colton to prom would lead to a happy ending.

But then my happy thoughts turned to dark scenarios of "What if...?"

> What if he gets a disgusted look on his face and says, "No!"

> What if he blabs at school, and everyone finds out I asked a boy to prom? Will people think I'm desperate?

> Even worse, what if everyone finds out I was rejected by a sophomore?

If rejection was my #1 fear, then my #2 fear was public embarrassment. In the worst-case scenario, asking Colton to prom ended with the entire school making fun of me and being known as the girl who got rejected. My reputation would be ruined. My fears screamed at me, "Don't do it! It's not worth the risk."

Do I listen to the voice inside my head that tells me to go after what I want, or do I listen to the voice that tells me to play it safe?

I had a choice to make.

I decided I couldn't let my fears control my life or my behavior. Playing it safe was the easy choice, but I would be giving up what I wanted. If I didn't take a risk, I had no shot at the reward.

Rather than focusing on my fears, I focused on what success would look like—slow dancing at prom with my handsome date. This was my opportunity to do something to make my vision come true. I listened to the voice in my head that said, "Colton would make an amazing prom date. He doesn't seem the type to blab. You have to ask him. There is a chance he will say, "Yes!""

It still took me several weeks to act on my decision to ask Colton to prom. Either I was too nervous or the perfect opportunity to ask him never presented itself. Either there were too many witnesses, or I didn't know how to bring it up smoothly in conversation.

I stressed and agonized about the when and the how of asking him. One Saturday morning at work, with prom just around the corner, I had run out of time. It was now or never. On my break, I looked for Colton up and down the aisles and found him stocking milk by himself. This was it. I forced the words out of my mouth.

"Hey, how's it going?" I said. "I have something to ask you. Would you be interested in going to prom with me?"

I braced myself for his answer.

"No, sorry, I can't," he replied. "I'm not going to prom with anyone."

I was crushed. I walked away sad and disappointed by his response. But I felt something else too. I felt good about myself. I was proud that I did what I told myself I would do. I did something that took a lot of guts and didn't give in to my fears. When it came to self-trust, I leveled up in a big way. It felt good to know I could follow through on hard things.

The experience grew my confidence. I knew what it felt like to do something that scared me to death. The thought of rejection was slightly less scary because I had survived it. I knew I could ask a guy out again if I liked him enough.

Fast forward two years later to my first year in college. I met a young man named Kevin. I liked him a lot and tried to let him know with all types of flirting. But he wasn't picking up on any of my signals. This guy was clueless!

I realized I needed to be more direct in letting him know I was into him. I sent him a signal he couldn't miss. I sat on his lap. That definitely caught his attention!

Kevin asked me to his fraternity's date party soon after that. It became our first date, and a few months later, we became an exclusive couple. Nine years later, we said, "I do." When people ask me how we met, I tell them I made the first move.

Years later, my husband admitted that until I sat on his lap, he had no idea I liked him. I'm so glad I took matters into my own hands and didn't leave things up to him.

Fear of rejection is natural, but giving in to that fear is not natural.

Fear should never dictate your life. Fear should not hold you back from going after what you want. Fear should never limit your possibilities. Ask that special person on a date. Apply for that dream job. Go after that new client.

You may ask yourself, "What if it goes wrong?" But the more important question is, "What if it goes right?"

 You create a life based on the actions that you take.

Don't be afraid of being told, "No." Go after what you want. Grab the handles to doors of opportunities and start yanking them open.

KNOW WHAT YOU REALLY WANT

Desire is a powerful motivator. It gives a person the energy to move toward the object of their desire. The bigger the desire, the bigger the motivation.

Manifesting is the practice of thinking aspirational thoughts with the goal of making them real. The idea behind manifesting is that you create what you think and feel. Manifesting begins with knowing exactly what you want.

That's why it is critical to think about your deepest desires and the reasons behind them. Use everything you learned about yourself and what is important to you in Step #1: Create Clarity to help you answer these questions:

- *Why is this outcome important to me?*
- *What do I gain by getting it?*
- *What do I lose by not getting it?*
- *What happens if I do nothing?*
- *What am I willing to sacrifice to get it?*

 Know what you really want and own it.

When you know something is enormously important, you feel more confident about going after it. When something is clearly worth it, you will do whatever it takes to get it.

Let me give you an example. Near the end of high school, I took a blank page in my journal and made a list of all the qualities I wanted in my future husband. It was a long list that took up almost the entire page. I looked at it, and it was abundantly clear that I was picky. Very picky. I wondered if I could find someone who met all of my requirements. I realized there was a good chance I wouldn't, which meant I might never marry because I wasn't going to settle for just any husband. I decided that I would rather be happily unmarried than unhappily married.

I carried that list around in my head. When I met Kevin, my future husband, and we started dating and getting to know each other well, I started mentally checking things off that list. One day, he showed up in workout clothes and said he had come straight from playing basketball at the gym. Athletic. Check! Health-conscious. Check! Finding the right partner is much easier when you know what qualities you seek in someone. Kevin definitely measured up to my list, so I felt confident in making my move. The rest, as they say, is history.

Clarity in what you really want, whether in a romantic partner, a career, or something else, will help you achieve your heart's desire. You will narrow down your choices because it will be evident not everyone and everything is a great fit for you. You will make decisions that directly align with your goals. You will be motivated to go after what you want instead of waiting for someone or something to happen.

A friend once told me there is little difference between asking someone out and making a business pitch. The only difference is the product being sold. Whether it's someone agreeing to a date with you or agreeing to give you a business loan, a single yes could make your greatest desires come true!

 Figure out what you really want and make your move.

 **TIME TO CLIMB**

Make your move.

Think of someone you want to get to know better, either personally or professionally. Contact this person and ask them to coffee, a date, or a meeting. Take the pressure off. Think of it as a little experiment just to see what happens.

To get yourself in the proper mindset, answer the following questions beforehand:

> *What do I want to get out of making my move?*

> *What positive benefits come from asking, even if they say no?*

> *If they say yes, what good things will I tell myself?*

> *If they say no, what good things will I tell myself?*

MAKE CONFIDENT DECISIONS

A key component of confidence is the ability to trust your decisions. Despite uncertainty, you need to be able to trust your judgment and trust that you can handle the outcomes of your decisions. You accept that whatever happens, you will deal with it and move on.

People who can't make up their minds go through a lot of anxiety and stress. They spend time worrying about the unknown, and their indecisiveness leads to missed opportunities. Here are some common reasons why people can't make confident decisions and how to overcome them:

1) **Not understanding what is important to them.**
   They can't make up their mind because they don't know who they are and what they want in life. Lewis Carroll's often-quoted saying sums it up perfectly: "If you don't know where you're going, any road will do."

   That is why creating clarity is the first step to creating confidence. Knowing your core values, personal mission statement, goals, strengths, love language, etc. all serve to filter your choices so you can make decisions that directly align with what truly matters to you.

 A clear understanding of yourself creates a clear path forward.

2) **Scared of making the wrong decision and the potential negative consequences.**
   It's the common fear of "What if...?" Every decision has potential downsides, so it's important to focus on the upsides while creating the right mindset for dealing with any potential downsides.

   When making a decision, you must balance emotions with rational thinking. Create a list of pros and cons on paper. Physically writing the list down allows you to come back to it and make edits. When you see in black and white that the pros outweigh the cons, you can trust that you're making the right decision.

At the same time, think through any potential negative consequences of a decision and what you would do should they happen. Thinking ahead of the possibilities and coming up with a plan allows you to process your fear in a constructive way.

For example, when my husband and I made the big decision to move our family to a new city where we didn't know a single person, I thought to myself, "What if we end up hating it and regretting our decision?" It was a scary thought, but the solution was pretty simple. We could always sell our home and move back. Nearly every decision is reversible. At the same time, every decision is an opportunity for learning, experience, and growth, whether it goes the way you planned or not. Definitely write that down in the pro column!

Fear of the unknown is natural. It's how you respond to your fears that matters.

 Manage fears by planning for what could go wrong and what could go right.

3) **Overanalyzing to the point of indecision.** Considering something in detail and from different angles is a good thing, but not when it causes analysis paralysis. I have known people who

couldn't make a decision because they had too much information. I've also known people who couldn't make a decision because they didn't have enough information. There are also people who can't make a decision because they see both sides and are torn.

External research and information don't always make a hard decision easier. When this happens, it's time to get back to the basics. You need to answer two internal questions while considering the information you have available.

1. *What will solve your problem(s)?*

2. *What is in your control?*

For example, when deciding what type of business I wanted to start, I went through some analysis paralysis. There were many factors to consider, and I had a variety of interests and skills. What ultimately helped me decide was knowing I needed to select a business model that allowed me to achieve my career and financial goals while still having quality time with my family. I also understood that how hard I worked and my income potential were all in my control.

Once you know the answers to these two questions, go ahead and trust your gut instinct. Your feelings and intuition also exist to provide you with answers.

Combining your head with your heart leads to smart decisions you can trust.

Confident people take action even when they're not sure of the outcome. Since every decision comes with some level of uncertainty, all you can do is believe in yourself to handle what comes next.

 You don't need to feel 100% certain to feel confident.

REPLACE FEAR WITH TRUST

Rock climbing created a foundational shift in my mindset not once but twice. The second time happened when I rappelled for the first time. Rappelling is when a rock climber descends on the rope from the top of a rock face all the way to the bottom.

I gripped the rope attached to my carabiner. I inched backward with my feet towards the edge of the rock. As I moved closer and closer, butterflies swarmed in my stomach. My body temperature spiked. I stretched my neck to peek over the cliff at the ground dizzyingly far below.

My brain screamed, "No way you're doing that!"

What I was doing felt extremely dangerous. Human beings aren't supposed to go over the edge of a cliff on a rope! At the same time, I recognized that my fear wasn't based on any real danger. I was completely safe. I had already seen other people rappel down, and no dead or broken bodies were lying at the bottom.

But still, I almost chickened out if it hadn't been for my father coaching me.

"Grab the rope near your thigh with your right hand and grab the rope above your harness with your left hand."

I listened carefully and followed his instructions.

"Now, stand as close to the edge as possible. Feed the rope through with your right hand and start to lean back."

Lean back?! This felt wrong, like someone telling me to ride my bike backward. Why would any sane human purposefully lean backward over thin air?

I didn't want to do it. I was terrified. On the other hand, I trusted my father 100 percent to keep me safe.

I decided at that moment to put my faith in trust instead of listening to my fears.

Once I stopped listening to my fears, I could hear my inner voice more clearly.

"I want to do this. It looks fun and exciting!"

I slowly started leaning back. I made sure not to look down.

"Lean back some more," my father encouraged me.

I tilted back just a tiny bit more.

"Keep leaning back," he kept urging.

I leaned back a little bit more and then a little bit more again…

There I was, my tennis shoes gripping the edge of the rock and my entire body hovering in the air at a 45-degree angle. I'm doing it!

I started noticing the more I leaned back, the easier it was to feed the rope through my belay device and rappel down. By leaning further back, I could basically "walk" down the cliff face. The experience was both terrifying and satisfying. Why? Because I was the one making it happen. I was the one in control. I experienced the reward that came with taking a risk and pushing myself out of my comfort zone.

As a result of my choices that day, I grew in courage, confidence, and character. I learned the benefits of replacing fear with trust and how it changes a person's life.

 Fear holds you back, and trust propels you forward.

Trusting yourself and others will help you feel grounded when you're scared to fall or fail.

EXPAND YOUR COMFORT ZONE

Trying something new or different can make people feel stressed, anxious, and uncomfortable. People often avoid feelings of discomfort by staying within their comfort zone.

A person wants to apply for a new job but is concerned they're not qualified enough. They fear their application will get rejected. They decide not to apply so they no longer feel scared. A person has always dreamed of taking a solo vacation but worries about what could go wrong. They cancel their trip, so they no longer feel worried.

 The comfort zone may feel nice and safe, but it has a dark side.

By staying in your comfort zone, you settle for less when your life could be so much more. You will miss out on your biggest hopes and dreams. You will have regrets because you will always wonder, "What if...?"

What if you had applied for that job? How would your life or career be different? What if you had taken that solo vacation? What unforgettable memories would you have today?

It's said that life begins at the end of your comfort zone. Stepping outside the boundaries of what feels familiar is essential to living a full life. While it may feel very uncomfortable at first, it gets better the more you do it.

My adopted father took my siblings and me on numerous backpacking trips growing up. On those trips, it rained many times, and we had to hike and camp in cold conditions. The coldest I have ever been in my life was camping at an alpine lake in the Rocky Mountains. It rained every day, and I had to sleep each night in a soaked tent and a damp sleeping bag. Despite the rain on that trip, I still cherish memories of day hikes filled with majestic views and evenings spent singing songs around the campfire.

By not canceling those rainy trips, my father showed us that some things are worth doing even if they make us uncomfortable. He taught us not to be deterred by factors out of our control, such as the weather, and to make the best of a situation. He gifted us with an important life skill—learning how to deal with discomfort in a positive way.

Those trips with bad weather made my siblings and me tougher physically and mentally. They made us realize how much we could handle even as kids, and that grit mentality helped us take risks and face future challenges.

 Getting comfortable being uncomfortable expands your comfort zone.

Life will make you feel uncomfortable, but don't let that stop you. When you feel scared or anxious in a situation outside your comfort zone, do it anyway. More than likely, you will be grateful that you did.

 Fear is not an automatic stop sign.

You can still feel fear even when something is safe. In most cases, fear is a yield sign that means to proceed with care. You don't have to run away. You can choose to keep going.

Confidence doesn't come from doing things that are easy. The more you step outside your comfort zone, the more you will realize that you are much more capable than you ever believed. When that happens, you will see yourself in a whole new light—a person prepared to handle anything.

 ## TIME TO CLIMB

Get comfortable being uncomfortable.

Getting comfortable with being uncomfortable takes practice. It's a skill you can develop that helps expand your comfort zone. Use the following strategies to push your limits so you can grow in courage and confidence.

Sit with your feelings.

Remember the last time you were outside of your comfort zone. How did you feel? Think about the different feelings you experienced. Identify them, and name them. Were they positive, negative, or neutral? Acknowledge your feelings, and show yourself compassion for having them. Next, think about the physical sensations your feelings caused in your body and where you felt them. Breathe. Sit with your feelings, and don't push them away. It's healthy to feel all of your emotions, both pleasant and unpleasant. Try to understand your feelings and the reasons behind them. How did your feelings influence your actions?

Repeat this process of sitting with your feelings

and making sense of them every time you experience strong emotions in new situations.

Be curious about the unknown.

Instead of avoiding change or not trying something new because you're unsure what will happen, channel the Curious George in you. Curious George is a monkey and a loveable children's book character whose curiosity repeatedly gets him in trouble. But Curious George has a good heart and good intentions. By the end of every story, he always finds a way to turn his predicament into a positive experience. Recognize that your journey into the unknown is also a journey in personal growth and development.
Adopt the attitude that you are curious to know how it turns out!

Get out of your temperature comfort zone.

It's time to get out of your climate-controlled environments. Plan a fun activity where you have to be outside for a significant amount of time in either hot or cold weather that makes you physically uncomfortable. Embrace that your discomfort is making you stronger. Become a person who purposely does hard things because the outcome is worth it.

Dare to be different.

What if you stood out from the crowd instead of disappearing into it? What if when everyone else wears navy suits, you show up wearing your favorite brightly colored blazer? Pick a situation where you will dare to be different from the majority, either in how you look, what you say, or how you behave. Recognize the differences between what you anticipated happening and feeling versus what actually happened and how you felt. What did you learn about yourself from the experience?

Bond over being uncomfortable together.

Pick a fun activity you've been too scared to try and find a friend or group of people to do it with you who have never done it before either. Consider skydiving, taking an improv class, or doing another activity where fun and fear intersect. Be each other's biggest champion and cheerleader. With the right support, you can do anything!

MOVE PAST IMPOSTOR SYNDROME

A common thought that can rule us instead of fuel us is the belief that "I don't belong here." It's the idea that you don't deserve an opportunity or accolade because you aren't good enough or smart enough, even though your track record proves otherwise. You feel like a fraud and live in fear people will eventually figure it out for themselves.

This belief that you are not as competent as others perceive you to be is called impostor syndrome. It robs people of their confidence even when they've proved their competence.

What can you do to stop impostor syndrome?

The first thing you need to do is to stop comparing yourself to others. The feeling of not being smart enough or good enough often comes from assuming the other people in the room are smarter or better than you.

A second strategy is to keep showing up despite the self-doubt you feel. If you've been invited to sit at the table in the room where it happens, there is a good reason for it. Keep showing up. You'll start to understand why you were selected. Keep showing up, and the feeling of being an impostor will begin to diminish.

Years ago, LifeSquire owner Valerie Riley qualified to participate in a mastermind group for successful business owners with sales of above a million dollars. She was the first and only female in the group. As she attended meetings, she realized her peers did 10 times or more in sales than her company. One person had even sold a company for $100 million. In her mind, the group members were ridiculously more successful and further along in their business journey. She compared herself to them and thought, "What could they possibly learn from me?" She didn't believe she brought much value to the group. She felt like a complete impostor for two whole years.

Despite her feeling of inferiority, Valerie continued participating in all of their meetings. Her self-talk wouldn't let her quit. She told herself,

"You have to push through this. If you want to have a bigger, more successful company, you need to be around people who are 10 steps ahead of you."

For two years, she kept showing up. One day, the feelings of inferiority disappeared. How did that happen? Attending the meetings allowed her to see behind the curtain. She realized everyone in the group faced similar challenges and many of the same issues. They had more in common than she realized. As a result of her experience, Valerie no longer struggles with impostor syndrome. She said she can now walk into *any* room and not be intimidated by *anyone*.

 You are more capable than you think. Keep showing up, and you'll find this out for yourself.

USE BORROWED CONFIDENCE WHEN NECESSARY

Another valuable strategy to combat impostor syndrome is to use borrowed confidence. You can borrow from the confidence other people have in you. In other words, you can believe you have what it takes because other people believe you have what it takes.

When I was asked to emcee an event for the first time, it was for a large international energy company. Their event would take place over two days and have hundreds in attendance. I questioned if I could do the job well since I hadn't done this specific type of professional speaking before.

The person who asked me was my friend, Brian Ferrell, who owns the event and destination management company Factor110. A poor performance on my part would reflect badly on his reputation, as well as mine. The stakes were high, and I felt scared to say yes.

In this situation, I used borrowed confidence from Brian to influence my decision to say yes. His trust in my abilities bolstered my confidence and helped me overcome self-doubt.

I thought to myself, "If Brian believes that I can emcee this event, and he plans events for a living and is one of the best in his industry, then I will trust his judgment."

Brian's confidence in me led me to believe I could do the job successfully. With preparation, hard work, and rehearsals, I emceed the event in a way that convinced people I was an experienced emcee. The highest compliment I received came from an attendee who asked me afterward if I was using a teleprompter because I was so well-spoken. He was shocked when I told him there was no teleprompter.

Borrowing confidence gave me the push to try something new and different. In doing so, I discovered a new skill set. After that, I didn't need to use borrowed confidence anymore to trust I could be successful as an emcee.

When you borrow something, it's never supposed to be permanent. Borrowed confidence works well as a short-term strategy to help you get over a hump of self-doubt. It's necessary to utilize the other strategies outlined in this book that build long-term confidence.

Growing up, many of us relied on borrowed confidence from our parents and other trusted adults in our lives when it came to trying something new. We needed their belief in us in order to believe in ourselves. We listened to them when they told us, "You can do it!" Their words of encouragement and their unwavering confidence in our capabilities and potential made us see ourselves differently.

Even as an adult, you need people in your life who believe in you and push you to believe in yourself. Whether it's a friend, a family member, or a colleague, you need a support system of people who can boost your confidence when it's needed.

 No one is immune from self-doubt, and no one is 100% confident all the time.

Listen to the people who have confidence in you, and choose to believe what they say.

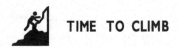 **TIME TO CLIMB**

Uncover your unique qualities and abilities.

There are people in your life who think you have many great qualities and abilities. Your goal is to discover what they are so you can be reminded of what makes you unique and capable.

Ask, text, or email the following question to at least three people you know:

What are some of my best qualities and greatest strengths?

Borrow confidence from these individuals and the positive things they say about you to do something outside of your comfort zone.

Fill in the blank:

I will borrow confidence from others and believe I can

_____.

DON'T MAKE NEGATIVE ASSUMPTIONS

When I moved to a different city in a new state, I needed to make some new friends. When I met people I liked, I would ask them if they wanted to meet for coffee or happy hour or join me for an activity. Some said yes, and some said no. For those who said they couldn't go, I didn't assume it was a rejection of me as a person. I didn't think to myself, "Was it because they didn't like me? Am I not interesting enough? Did I say something wrong?"

People will sometimes say "No" when you invite them out for coffee, ask them out on a date, apply for a new job, or try to make a sale. When you are rejected, even if it was done in the nicest way, it's natural to imagine all sorts of negative reasons why you were rejected. Those reasons often lead you to blame yourself because you assume they didn't think you were likable, attractive, intelligent, or accomplished enough. These types of thoughts cause you to take rejection personally and only make you feel worse. They're also not valid since they are based on assumptions.

 Negative assumptions are confidence killers.

Stop imagining negative reasons for why someone said no. If you can't help but make up reasons why, at least make positive assumptions such as:

- ☀ The person was busy.
- ☀ The person had a prior commitment.
- ☀ The person doesn't enjoy a particular activity.
- ☀ The person isn't ready for a relationship.
- ☀ The person had to choose from a lot of great applicants.
- ☀ The person doesn't have the money in their budget right now.

None of these reasons have anything negative to do with you. It's the difference between thinking thoughts that fuel you versus rule you. Positive thoughts will fuel you to keep making asks that lead to rewards.

I am enjoying the rewards of my new friendships and feel at home in my new community because I didn't take rejection personally.

What positive assumptions can help you overcome past rejections so you feel confident to make another ask?

GROW FROM FAILURES

When someone asked me to tell them about a time I failed, I couldn't think of a single example.

> Even though I ran for office and lost the election.

> Even though I started a business that wasn't profitable.

> Even though I co-wrote a children's story that didn't get published.

I can easily recall times I've lost, made huge mistakes, and didn't get what I worked for, but I don't consider any of them "failures. Some people might consider them failures. In my mind, they weren't failures because I learned something from them. They helped me grow into a person who is smarter, tougher, and better prepared. Although I didn't win or succeed, I became a better version of myself by doing them.

Failure is not failure if you learn from it.

For this reason, you don't need to be afraid of failing or making mistakes. Any lesson learned from an experience, whether good or bad, is a gift to your future self. You will become that much wiser. You will be able to make better decisions.

While I know what it feels like to lose publicly and fail to achieve a big goal, those aren't the outcomes I choose to focus on. By running for office and managing a campaign, I gained experience in fundraising, recruiting volunteers, designing flyers, and public speaking. By co-writing a children's story, I learned about the publishing world and attended a children's book writing conference. I plan on using the knowledge I acquired to create a new and improved version of that book. With all that I gained, there was no way I considered myself a "loser" or a "failure."

Often, you can learn more from your mistakes than your successes. Use that knowledge to try new ideas and approaches. Use what you learned about yourself to keep growing and evolving. Become version 2.0 of yourself and then version 2.1, 2.2, etc.

In Henry Ford's words, "Failure is only the opportunity to begin again more intelligently."

 **TIME TO CLIMB**

Determine your lessons learned.

What is something you did that didn't go according to plan that you or someone else might consider a "failure?" Think about everything you learned from not succeeding or getting what you wanted.

What are the Top 3 things you learned from that experience that will allow you to begin again more intelligently?

Top 3 Things You Learned From Failure

1.

2.

3.

Repeat this activity with other "failures," and start rewiring your mind to find your lessons learned.

REFRAME FEAR

A benefit of living in an industrialized nation is that the large majority of the population has access to water, food, housing, jobs, and transportation. Children can go to school for free, and police officers and firefighters work to keep people safe.

Most people can go about their daily lives without fearing for their lives or safety. However, that doesn't mean that most people don't live with fear. It's quite the opposite. Many people wrestle with a lot of fears that prevent them from finding true happiness and success.

Here are the most common fears people have:

Fear of Failure

The fear of not succeeding prevents people from even trying.

Fear of Rejection

The fear of being told "No" stops people from asking for something they want.

Fear of the Unknown

The fear of "What if…?" keeps people from taking a risk and going beyond their comfort zone.

Fear of Being Out of Your League

The fear of not being good enough or qualified enough stops people from going after something.

Fear of Loss

The fear of losing something we already have makes people avoid taking any risks. These things could be health, wealth, comfort, freedom, or reputation.

Fear of Judgment

Fear of what others will think or say keeps people from speaking up or taking action.

Fear of Not Being Perfect

Fear of making mistakes and not having all of the answers is similar to fear of failure and keeps people from trying something new.

Fear of Disappointment

Fear of unmet expectations or being let down keeps people from taking a chance.

Fear of the Worst Happening

Fear of their worst imagination coming true prevents people from seeing all of the potential good things that could happen.

These fears are not external threats, such as not having enough food or water. These fears exist only in a person's mind and often control how a person lives their life.

The reality is that many of these fears are unlikely to come true. They are imagined. If some were to come true, the consequences would most likely be short-lived and could be overcome.

Mistakes are almost never permanent nor fatal.

According to psychologists, people who let fear dominate their lives believe two things:

1. Bad things will happen. You will fail, you will be unlikeable, and you will put yourself or your loved ones in danger.

2. You won't be able to handle it. You'll be overwhelmed, alone, and helpless.

Bad things can and do happen, but calculated risks and well-thought-out decisions have a good chance of having positive outcomes. That's why it's called taking a risk and not taking a gamble.

It's important to keep fear in perspective by rationally thinking through the likelihood of a negative consequence you've imagined actually occurring.

My family went on many backpacking trips. As we hiked across the Chihuahuan Desert in Texas or into the San Juan Mountains in Colorado, there was a chance we could have gotten lost, fallen off a cliff, been bitten by a rattlesnake, or been attacked by bears. These fears definitely crossed my mind, but I didn't dwell on them. That's because my father told me something that has always helped me put my fears into perspective. He said,

"The most dangerous thing people do every day is get in a car."

It's true. Every day, people climb inside metal containers that go flying down the highway at 75 miles per hour, inches away from 25,000-pound 18-wheeler trucks. At any moment, a distracted driver, a drunk driver, or their own mistake could cause a major car accident.

Have you ever been tired and driven down the interstate at night? Most of us have, even though it's extremely dangerous. The combination of low mental alertness and low visibility while driving at high speeds can be deadly—for ourselves and the other drivers on the road.

Each year, 1.35 million people are killed on roadways around the world, according to the Centers for Disease Control and Prevention (CDC). In the United States, motor vehicle crashes are a leading cause of death and kill more than 100 people daily. Compare that with a person's chance of being mauled to death by a bear. The North American Bear Center states on its website that the 750,000 black bears in North America kill less than one person per year on average. I've met people who will not go camping for fear of being attacked by bears. Yet, almost everyone doesn't think twice about getting in a vehicle.

Another common fear that isn't rationally based is public speaking. The Chapman University Survey on American Fears found that public speaking is America's biggest phobia. Twenty-five percent of Americans are deathly afraid of speaking in front of a large group of people. Yet, there is nothing inherently dangerous about public speaking. While you could trip on stage and break a leg or the ceiling could come crashing down, these scenarios are highly unlikely to occur.

It is possible that your mind could go blank or you could give your entire presentation not realizing you have food stuck in your teeth. Yes, it would feel embarrassing, and some people may talk about it, but soon the audience will move on to something else and forget all about it.

In reality, people are too busy with their own lives to focus on yours for very long.

It's time to stop worrying about the "worst" and start thinking about the "best" that could happen. For instance, you could change someone's life!

Public speaking is simply sharing information or telling a story to an audience, often with the goal of helping those who are listening. Your likelihood of success—helping at least one person in the audience—is extremely high.

 Manage fear by keeping it in the proper perspective.

Ask yourself these questions to reframe your fears:

What is the likelihood my fear will come true exactly as I've imagined it?

What experiences, opportunities, or rewards will I gain by facing my fear?

What are some things I can do to make sure I take a smart and calculated risk?

 Fear and danger are not the same thing.

Fear is an emotional and physical reaction to danger. When the danger is real, such as getting too close to the fire or the edge of a cliff, fear can keep you alive and safe. When danger is perceived and fueled by imagination, fear harms you by preventing you from taking proper action.

The human body physically reacts to fear in the same way whether it's real or imagined with sweating, increased heart rate, and shortness of breath. Fear is fear to your body, but it shouldn't be to your mind. You must switch from reacting to responding. You must stop and analyze your fear, and make an intentional decision to disregard fear that isn't based on real danger.

Don't listen to lies, exaggerations, and doomsday stories that others tell you or that you tell yourself. Don't let your fears take away your power to act in your best interest. Trust that things will turn out okay.

 Let your dreams of success outshine your nightmares of failure.

Picture what is waiting for you on the other side of fear. Is it a dream job? A purpose-filled life? A loving partner? A powerful speech? A new invention? An exciting adventure?

If you look closely, the thing that awaits you is much bigger than your fear.

TURN BAD EXPERIENCES INTO A FORCE FOR GOOD

Life is rarely binary. The only outcomes aren't win or lose, success or failure. Much of life is a mixture of good and bad, which means you can always find the good in the bad.

Take sports for example. Losing a hard-fought game after giving it your all shouldn't make you feel like a loser. You can take pride in your effort and teamwork. You can learn from the experience and use it to improve. You can feel like a winner even when the scoreboard doesn't show it.

When things don't go your way, you get to decide how you respond. You get to choose how it influences your future. Do you look for the message in the mess? Do you work hard to find the rainbow after the storm?

 Use a negative experience to fuel you forward.

My friend, Cathy Cummings, is an accomplished business owner and public servant. While operating a highly successful restaurant, she ran for lieutenant governor of the State of Oklahoma and later went on to serve as mayor of the City of The Village. Cathy's campaign for lieutenant governor at the age of 53 was her very first time running for public office.

When she was a single mother of three young girls, she worked three jobs to support her family. One of those jobs was as a waitress. During that time, Cathy started dating the brother of a good friend. He seemed like a wonderful man and a good father to his children. She enjoyed their budding relationship until she saw a different side of him on a joint family beach vacation. She noticed that every morning he poured himself a tall glass of alcohol, and he kept pouring himself drinks throughout the day. After a few days, she pointed out his excessive drinking and told him she wasn't comfortable with it, especially with both sets of their children around. He became irate and started making personal attacks on her.

He yelled in her face, "You are never going to be anything more than a f***ing waitress until the day you die." Cathy ended the relationship that day, but his spiteful words never left her. She said his words lit a fire inside her that has never stopped burning.

"That was the catalyst to everything I've done this far in my life," Cathy said. "I wasn't going to be just a f***ing waitress.'" She was going to be a person who made her life count, no matter what.

Cathy ran for Lieutenant Governor in her very first election. Her lack of campaign experience and the fear of the unknown didn't stop her. She listened to the people around her who told her she could figure it out with preparation and hard work.

"Confidence comes from walking through that fear," she said. "Walk through that fear to get where you need to be."

When people told Cathy she had no business running for office, she didn't believe them. She focused on her desire to serve and believed by winning the election, she could improve the lives of Oklahoma families and small business owners.

Sometimes lack of confidence comes from believing the lies and limitations people tell you about your worth or your abilities. When someone tells you that you're not smart enough, experienced enough, man enough, or anything else negative, they are only giving their opinion.

 Never take someone's opinion of you as fact.

Don't let what people say or think hold you back. According to Cathy,

> *"The only thing that comes from not trying is regret."*

When it comes to building your confidence, Cathy gives two pieces of advice. The first one is finding the fire inside you that drives you forward and keeping it alive. The second one is finding someone who can help you walk through your fear because everyone needs a cheerleader.

As Cathy has demonstrated by how she lives her life, a bad experience doesn't have to define a person or crush their self-confidence. It can be a source of strength and a driving force for good.

 **TIME TO CLIMB**

Propel yourself forward.

Negative life experiences can either break you or make you stronger. They can either hold you back or push you to do great things. Often, the determining factor is not the event itself, but how you perceive it and respond to it.

Use the following journal prompts to flip your narrative around a negative experience in your life so it propels you forward instead of holding you back.

> *Write about a negative experience and how it affected you.*
>
> *What can your future self take away from this experience that is valuable?*
>
> *In what ways are you stronger or smarter today than when this experience occurred?*
>
> *You cannot control the past. What can you control moving forward that will lead to positive results?*
>
> *What will help you process your emotions around this? Where can you get the help and healing you need?*

Despite this negative experience in your life, what is your hope for your future? What steps will you take to make it happen?

MOVE FROM WORRYING TO LEARNING

Have you ever put something off you didn't want to do and paid for it with constant worry?

When I was about 12 years old, my adopted mother gave me the name and phone number of our family dentist's office and told me I needed to make my own appointment. What?! I didn't want to talk to a strange adult on the phone! None of my friends had to make their own appointments!

"Why do I have to be the one to do it?" I whined. She told me it was because I knew my schedule better than anyone else. I was so scared and nervous that I put off the dreaded task for days. I was worried I wouldn't know the right thing to say. Plus, I was hoping my mother would change her mind and make the appointment for me, but she never did.

I was tired of constantly worrying about it and how that weighed on me. One day after school, I made myself pick up the phone to make the call and get it over with. The receptionist I talked to was friendly, and I was off the phone in a few short minutes. Unlike what I had imagined, it wasn't bad at all! I hung up the phone feeling proud of myself. I felt responsible and mature after having a grown-up conversation. That moment changed me. I felt more confident because I was a kid doing grown-up things. I wasn't afraid to have phone conversations with adults anymore after that. Thanks Mom!

Most of the time, when something scares you, what you imagine is far worse than the actual experience. You spend days or weeks worrying about how terrible something will be, and it generates more negative feelings. You're causing yourself unnecessary pain.

"We suffer more in imagination than in reality."

– SENECA

Those negative feelings and thoughts of worst-case scenarios won't go away until the deed is done. Once you face what scares you, you can move on, learn from the experience, and do better next time.

 By taking action, you move from worrying about it to learning from it.

Think of challenging experiences as rings on a tree. With every challenge, you grow a new ring that makes you stronger and wiser.

Key Points of Step #2: Create Self-Trust

- ☀ Accept your unique tastes
- ☀ Keep promises to yourself
- ☀ Grow from mistakes and failures
- ☀ Focus on thoughts that fuel you

STEP #3: CREATE TO CREATE CONFIDENCE

**"Confidence is not something you have.
It's something you create."**

- Tony Robbins

Diana Rogers Jaeger

The sun is powerful and a force for good. It radiates light, heat, and energy, making life on Earth possible. It's beautiful. The colors it generates during sunrise and sunset will take your breath away. The sun is strong and long-lasting. Not even the darkest clouds can keep the sun from shining. Every day it rises to create a new day with new possibilities.

 When you have confidence, you create your own sunshine.

Just as the sun can't stop itself from sharing its light and energy with the world, neither can a confident person. You will radiate an energy and glow that draws people in. You will stand out because you shine so brightly.

Many people think they need confidence *before* they can do certain things.

> *I need more confidence before I can do that.*

> *I don't have the confidence to try that.*

> *I'm not confident enough to face my fears.*

I'll let you in on a big secret:

 You don't need confidence to take action. You take action to create confidence.

I truly mean "create" confidence.

Definition of Create:

To make or bring into existence; to cause to happen as a result of one's actions.

When you create, you are the source and cause of something new. You will realize you have the power to bring thoughts and ideas into existence and to make things happen. Through the process of creating, you start to appreciate your qualities and abilities.

 Creating confidence for yourself will transform your present and your future.

It will change your outlook on life and lead you to consistently act on what matters to you.

Confidence begins with Step #1: Creating Clarity and Step #2: Creating Self-Trust. But Step #3: Create to Create Confidence gets you to the point where you are living and breathing confidence!

 Creating requires taking action.

You can't live life from the sidelines. You can't become confident from wishing and hoping and thinking and praying. You have to get out there and give something a try!

"Action is a great restorer and builder of confidence. Inaction is not only the result, but the cause of fear."

– NORMAN VINCENT PEALE

The fears that fill your mind will stay there and possibly even grow unless you do something to challenge their existence. If your fear tells you, "Don't do it. You'll embarrass yourself," you must take action to prove it wrong. You could study harder, practice harder, or talk to an expert to increase your chances of success. Then you do it and see what happens because the most valuable lessons are experienced first-hand.

Take driving a car, for example. You can watch videos on how to drive, watch someone else drive, or use a driving simulator, but they won't compare to the real thing. While you can learn and prepare as much as possible beforehand, nothing teaches you better than actual driving experience. Although it can be scary, it takes getting behind the wheel to know what it's really like. Practically everyone I know has a driver's license. That means they didn't let their fear of having a car accident stop them from learning to drive and continuing to drive.

As people gain lots of experience, driving can become second nature to the point that people sometimes drive home on autopilot. They're acting without thinking about what they are doing. That's a long way from the anxious, terrified teenager most of us were the first time we got behind the wheel.

 Think of your life experiences, both the good and the bad, as practice for what comes next.

The more first-hand experiences you participate in and learn from, the more prepared you will be to handle what life throws at you. As a result, your fears will shrink, and your confidence will naturally grow.

CREATE DON'T CONSUME

In the world we live in, it's far too easy to consume. Movies and TV shows can be streamed and binge-watched instantly. Books can be downloaded and read immediately. People can buy what they want 24/7 from stores and restaurants and have it delivered within minutes, hours, or a few days.

We've been raised to be consumers. Marketing messages train us from birth to think that consuming goods and services is necessary for achieving well-being and happiness. The media tells the public that buying more, newer, and better makes someone a good citizen because they contribute to a strong economy. If you believe advertisements, there is a product for every problem. Feeling down? Buy this pill. Looking for romance? Buy this dating app. Hate shopping? Buy this subscription box. Lack of confidence? Buy these clothes, make-up, and weight-loss products. The idea being marketed is that confidence is based on appearance. Don't buy into that idea. It's a short-term gimmick.

 You can't consume your way to confidence.

Consuming products to make you feel good about yourself doesn't create confidence that lasts. True confidence is built from the inside out and doesn't go away. Your confidence shouldn't disappear from a bad hair day, a negative experience, or a cruel comment.

 You have the power to create unlimited confidence.

This chapter makes it simple by taking you through a variety of first-hand experiences that show you how to do it. Each one will challenge you to grow in new and different ways. By doing them, your courage and hard work will be rewarded. As you take action, the confidence you create will become an integral part of who you are—your mindset, your self-identity, and your behaviors. You will BE confident.

DARE TO DO SOMETHING FUN AND SCARY

New experiences lead to self-discovery. Afterward, you see yourself differently. Your mind has been altered, and you will never be the same. After trying something new, you may realize you are an adrenaline junkie or have certain strengths.

Remember as a kid when people would dare you to do something? You probably did some of them. Dares push people to go outside their comfort zone and do something they would never do on their own.

I remember in grade school when a classmate dared me to ride my bicycle down an alley full of loud, barking dogs. Challenge accepted. I pedaled my little legs as fast as they could go. Dogs on my left and right started barking their heads off and jumping on the chain-link fences. My heart pounded in my chest because it sounded like they would hop the fence and bite me! I made it to the end of the alley, and I started laughing. That dare tested my courage, and I won! It taught me that overcoming fear can be exciting and rewarding.

 When you try something new, you give yourself a chance to prove your fears wrong.

Most adults don't usually go around daring each other, and that's a good thing. Negative peer pressure is unhealthy and can even be dangerous. However, many adults could benefit from a good dare—positive peer pressure in the form of motivation and encouragement.

What if people who cared about you dared you to do something they knew would be good for you? What would that experience be?

It's probably something they know scares you or makes you uncomfortable, but doing it will lead to something positive in your life.

Would they require you to speak up for yourself, ask for a raise, or take that job in a new city? Would they push you to finally do the thing you've always wanted to do but have never done? Is there something fun and scary that they would pressure you to try?

Scuba diving fell into the fun and scary category for me. Getting to explore the ocean and seeing marine life up close excited me, but I was scared of all the things that could go wrong. The main one was sharks! For you, it could be ziplining or taking an improv class. Maybe it's signing up for Toastmasters classes or training for your first 5K race.

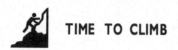 **TIME TO CLIMB**

Commit to trying something fun and scary in the next month to create a new experience for yourself.

You may end up finding your spark, a new passion, or a new friend!

Find a partner who can hold you accountable to make sure you actually do it. It needs to be someone you don't want to disappoint and who won't take your excuses. Focus on the good things that will happen from trying this new thing—the excitement of the experience and all that you'll learn.

Do what you tell yourself you will do, and you will create self-trust. The end result is that you will have the confidence to achieve whatever you set your mind to.

One of the people I admire most said this about new experiences:

"If you want something you never had, you must be willing to do something you've never done."

– THOMAS JEFFERSON

LEARN FROM NEW EXPERIENCES

For children, almost every experience is new.

The first day of school. The first day of soccer team practice. The first airplane ride. The first sleepover. The first time riding a roller coaster. The first time performing on stage. Each of these firsts can strike feelings of worry, nervousness, and fear in a child. But they do it anyway!

As a result, they come out the other side a little bit wiser about the world and themselves.

If children refused to try anything new or if the adults in their lives didn't introduce them to new experiences, their development would be stunted. They would miss out on many opportunities to learn valuable life lessons that build their confidence. It's why many parents intentionally register their children for different sports, activities, and camps so they can try new things, develop new skills, and learn what they like and don't like.

 Every new experience is a learning experience.

Trying new things can be challenging, but they push you to grow. In many cases, the harder the experience, the bigger the lessons and the more they stick with you.

When my youngest son was in kindergarten and learning to read, he brought a set of sight words flash cards home each week. When he struggled to read through a brand-new set of sight words, he wanted to quit right away. He would flail his little body in his chair or throw himself on the rug and moan, "It's too hard! I'll never get it right!"

On the second and third days of practicing his sight words, he continued complaining that they were too hard. We kept practicing them together. By the fourth or fifth day, he knew most, if not all of the words, and he suddenly stopped complaining.

If it were up to my son, he would have quit on the first try. But as his parent, I couldn't let him. It was vital for him to learn to read and see for himself how effort and practice pay off. Week after week of trying and practicing, I watched him gradually improve at reading.

 Practice leads to competence and confidence.

After a few months, he stopped saying things like, "I'll never learn these," when he brought home a new set of words. He knew firsthand it wasn't true. His experience taught him he can learn new things and that hard things get easier the more you do them.

What childhood experiences pushed you to learn, grow, and become more confident? What new experiences could cause similar things to happen to you now?

You can only become the person you want to be through personal growth and development. Embrace new experiences. Don't avoid a good challenge or quit when things get difficult. Welcome the opportunity to gain new knowledge, skills, and insight.

However, just as you would show patience to a child doing something for the first time, be patient with yourself when trying something new. Show yourself love and empathy. Provide yourself with lots of encouragement. You will come out the other side stronger and wiser.

 ## TIME TO CLIMB

Commit to trying a new experience that you will use to learn and grow.

What new experience will you try and what do you hope to learn from it?

Ask yourself the following questions afterward to help you discover the valuable lessons you gained.

What did I learn about the world?

What did I learn about myself?

What did I learn that was useful?

What did I learn that will stick with me?

CREATE A SUCCESS LIST

Do you appreciate all of the amazing things you have accomplished in your life?

If you don't, it's time to walk down memory lane. Remembering your past moments of triumphs and achievements benefits your mental and emotional health. By reliving them in your mind, you can once again experience the happy emotions you felt. You will feel like you are coming off a win! It's much easier to feel confident when you feel good about yourself and the things you've done.

Don't take your past successes for granted. They serve as hard evidence of what you can do.

What memories are you most proud of?

Start with your early childhood. Do you remember when you learned to tie your shoes or scored your first goal? As a teenager, can you recall a time that you stood up to a bully or volunteered for a leadership role? Do you remember how proud you were as an adult when you graduated college, nailed a big project, or raised your children to be kind?

These kinds of moments need to be pulled from your memory and brought to the forefront of your mind. You need to create a success list. A success list includes key moments from your life that remind you of your many capabilities and accomplishments. Remembering them will boost your self-confidence and help you channel past successes into new successes.

 Cultivating a success mindset goes hand in hand with cultivating a confidence mindset.

 **TIME TO CLIMB**

Create a success list by jotting down three or more accomplishments in multiple areas of your life.

Use the following categories below to get you started. Feel free to skip or add categories as needed.

Personal/Individual

Family/Friends

Career/Job

Health/Sports

Hobbies

Financial

Spiritual

Volunteer

Other _____

CREATE A POSITIVE HABIT

You have so much to do every day that wouldn't it be nice to accomplish something without thinking much about it? What if you ate fresh fruits or vegetables with every meal? What if you started every day by making your bed?

Habits are repeated behaviors that are nearly or completely involuntary. Positive habits are powerful because they make your life better without much effort.

 Creating positive habits, no matter how tiny, builds self-trust.

Trust is built by repeatedly doing what you say you will do. You prove to yourself you have the determination and the discipline to stick with things that matter. Strong habits develop a strong mindset that leads you to believe in yourself. If you can stick with eating breakfast every day to improve your energy level or calling your mom or dad each week to keep your relationship strong, you can trust yourself to do other things that take effort and self-discipline to accomplish.

Research shows it takes an average of 66 days to form a habit. Sometimes it takes less time, and sometimes it takes longer. The length of time shouldn't matter if you're focused on the outcome. Building a habit is not a race. Steady progress is how new behaviors gradually become automatic.

Habits may not be easy to form, but the habits themselves and the process you go through in developing good habits can be life-changing. Positive habits build confidence because they demonstrate that you are in control of your life.

 When you begin to automatically trust yourself, you develop the habit of feeling confident.

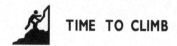 ## TIME TO CLIMB

Develop a new habit that will significantly improve the quality of your life.

In what ways will forming this habit make your life easier or better?

What baby steps will you take this week to start repeating this behavior?

What will you do to keep your promise to yourself to develop this positive habit?

Who will you make your accountability partner?

IMPACT SOMEONE'S LIFE

Volunteering is one of the most rewarding experiences a person can have. It's freely giving your time and labor to benefit others in big and small ways. You can not only change a person's life while doing it, but you can also change yours.

According to the Mayo Clinic Health System, volunteering improves mental and physical health, provides a sense of purpose, and nurtures friendships. As is typical with volunteering, you receive a lot more than you give. In addition to positively impacting your community, you gain new skills and experiences and increase your life satisfaction.

Volunteering boosts your confidence.

After graduating college, I started volunteering as a troop leader for Girl Scouts Western Oklahoma, where I mentored girls and took them camping to build their confidence and leadership skills. I later served on its board of directors as an executive committee member and then as board chair. During that time, I helped raise money for scholarships and capital campaigns, and I served on the committee that oversaw the construction of the organization's new urban camp and STEM Center called Camp Trivera.

My volunteer work with Girl Scouts allowed me to follow my passions and make a difference in the lives of others. Along the way, I gained valuable experience in many areas, such as strategic planning and policy making.

I also served my profession through various leadership positions, including president of the local International Association of Business Communicators (IABC) chapter. In these volunteer roles, I developed many of the leadership and management skills I have today. For example, understanding how to motivate and lead volunteers, individuals who aren't paid or required to do their work, prepared me to be a leader who doesn't need to use their position or authority to be effective.

Volunteering increased my confidence because I felt good about myself, I felt good helping others, and I felt good that I was learning new skills.

Volunteering can do the same things for you. It's an opportunity to use your talents and feel a sense of accomplishment. It gives you the chance to meet people from all walks of life while gaining a variety of life experiences.

 It's easier to see your true worth when serving others.

 TIME TO CLIMB

Volunteer your time to make an impact in someone's life.

Determine how you want to make a difference, and choose a volunteer assignment that aligns with your passion or personal mission statement.

After volunteering, journal about your experience.

What did you enjoy?

What knowledge or skills did you learn or put to use?

What impact did you make in the lives of others?

How did the experience change the way you see yourself?

TALK TO PEOPLE WHO HAVE FOUND SUCCESS

When you have a goal or a dream you want to achieve, there is no use in reinventing the wheel and trying to figure things out on your own. There are people who have the knowledge and experience you seek who can help you get to your goal much faster and easier.

The best people to talk to are those who have already found success in your field.

They can share their path to success and offer advice on what to do and what to avoid. They can also give you honest feedback on your ideas and plans.

The first business I started offered gift consulting services. It was a side gig I was trying to turn into a profitable business that could meet my financial goals. I spent a lot of time researching gift consulting businesses and how to grow a business, but I couldn't find the answers I needed.

Then I remembered an article I had read in a local business publication about an entrepreneur named Valerie Riley. I admired the way she had grown her personal assistant business from scratch. I knew I could learn a lot from her. I didn't know if I had a viable business model with my gift consulting service, and I needed guidance from someone with business experience.

I found Valerie's email address on her company website and sent her a message asking if I could take her to lunch. She agreed, and during our lunch meeting, she graciously listened to my problem and openly shared her experience and advice with me.

The Internet is incredibly useful for researching, but you can't ask Google, "What do you think of my idea?" or "What should be my next step?" I could ask Valerie those questions. I learned a lot from her during our first conversation, and, afterward, she offered to meet with me every few weeks.

Valerie helped me think like a strategic business owner and inspired me to keep pursuing my entrepreneurial goals. She influenced my decision to go in a new direction and create my current company, Love To Appreciate Consulting. Talking with her fueled my mind and my spirit.

There are many successful people like Valerie who enjoy helping others. They can answer your questions and help you become more confident in your decisions. I call them "dream helpers." They are out there waiting for you to introduce yourself.

 Increase your chances of succeeding by talking to people who have already found success.

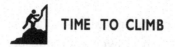 TIME TO CLIMB

Meet with someone who has found success in your field.

Create an opportunity to learn from them by inviting them to coffee, lunch, or a video call. Don't be afraid of being told no. Assume people want to help because it's true. Most people want to pay their success forward and feel honored when asked to share their knowledge. If they can't meet with you, ask them for the name of someone else they recommend you talk to and invite that person.

CREATE YOUR OWN VERSION

The act of creating builds confidence in your ideas and abilities. However, when it comes to creating, you might think, "Someone else has already come up with my idea," or "Someone else already does it better, so why bother?".

Should Dave Thomas not have created Wendy's just because McDonald's already existed? Should the creators of Uber not have started their company just because Zimride already existed?

When my children draw pictures of characters they've copied from a book or a video game, I don't stop them because they're not creating something original. I celebrate their creation which started as a blank piece of paper. I encourage them to keep drawing whatever inspires them.

When you create, it is 100% your creation.

It doesn't matter if it's original or not. It's yours. No one will have done it exactly like you.

At the time this book was written, a search for "confidence book" in the Books section of the Amazon website revealed 60,000 results. That didn't stop me from writing my own book on confidence. My personality, life experiences, and the people I've gotten to know and learn from have all influenced my point of view on how to create confidence. I can use what I know to help others.

There are a million ways to create. Let your imagination run wild. It doesn't matter what anyone else has done before you. What matters is connecting with yourself and using the power of your mind, body, and emotions to create something new to you.

 ## TIME TO CLIMB

Pick a passion project and create your own version of something.

It could be art, writing, cooking or baking, a DIY project, crafting, a video, or anything else you enjoy. The important thing is to finish it and feel the satisfaction of creating.

Afterward, take some time for self-reflection, and journal about the following:

What did you gain from the creating experience?

In what ways did the act of creating affect your mind, body, and emotions?

What did the act of creating do for your self-confidence?

TAKE A SINGLE STEP FORWARD

Hiking is walking with a destination. The destination could be anywhere, such as a meadow, a lake, or the top of a mountain. Getting to any destination requires the same thing—taking one step forward at a time.

Hiking is my favorite outdoor activity. If I want to really challenge myself, I like to hike a "Fourteener." Fourteeners are mountains that are more than 14,000 feet above sea level. There are more than 50 Fourteeners in the state of Colorado. Looking up at a Fourteener is both inspiring and daunting. You take in all of its grandeur but question whether you can physically reach the top.

Thinking of a big dream or goal feels the same way. It's exciting to think of what it would feel like to achieve it, but you wonder if it's even possible.

Much like hiking, success is incremental. One step after another adds up to a mile, and every mile gets you closer to your destination.

 Every step forward is a small success.

Some individuals can hike to the summit of a Fourteener in a few hours, while others require the greater part of a day. Either way, everyone makes it to the summit by taking one step at a time. There is no elevator to the top of a mountain, and there is no elevator to success.

When you view success as an elevator, you create unrealistic expectations that put pressure on you to make it to the top quickly or on the first try. That type of pressure can diminish your confidence and motivation.

Many people have an idea for a new product or service and want to take it to market. But they never try to do it. Why? Most likely, they're afraid it won't be successful, and they won't make enough money. For them, the risk is too high.

But what if the stakes weren't all or nothing? What if the stakes were incremental? What if someone made it their goal to help just one person with their new product? Or to help 10 people with their new service? What next step could they take to make that happen? Is it possible to create a single prototype? Could they offer 10 free trials of their new service to target customers?

Either of those steps would take someone closer to turning their idea into reality. When you want to accomplish something big, get rid of any unnecessary pressure that doesn't fuel you forward to your goal.

 By taking one step after another in the right direction, you can get to where you want to go or someplace better than you imagined.

Major General Rita Aragon was inducted into the Oklahoma Hall of Fame in 2016. I got to know her when we served together on the board of directors of Girl Scouts Western Oklahoma. Her story is incredible.

Rita enlisted in the U.S. Air National Guard as an Airman Basic at the age of 32. As a science teacher and single mother of two young girls, she needed additional income to support her family. Taking advantage of every opportunity, she climbed up the military ranks to become a two-star general. In the process, she broke many glass ceilings. Rita became the first female in the Air National Guard to hold the rank of brigadier general and the first woman in the United States to command a state's Air National Guard.

Although it may not seem like it, Rita's rise to success was gradual. She didn't become a general overnight. In fact, she applied three times before being accepted into Officer Candidate School.

"There is no magic pill to become general," she said. "It was painful, long, and grueling to get there."

When she joined the Air National Guard, Rita had no prior military experience. That didn't stop her. She looked at her teaching experience and her college degree as an advantage. Her competence in those areas gave her self-confidence.

She started taking on responsibilities and enrolling in classes that prepared herself for the next rank up. There were no shortcuts or skipping steps. Rita said she kept working her way up one task, one class, and one rank at a time.

In her courses, she witnessed grown men who were much taller and stronger want to throw up at the thought of speaking in front of a group. She stood out among her peers because public speaking didn't intimidate her. It's not that she was a natural at doing it. As a teacher, she had many years of experience speaking every single day in front of people—her students!

"Public speaking is a skill," Rita said. "You learn by doing, like tying your shoe."

New skills get easier the more they are practiced. Every success, no matter how small, acts as a stepping stone, and every experience builds a person's confidence in tackling the next level.

"There is no need to jump into the deep end," Rita explained.

"You gain confidence and competence by doing something a little at a time."

As she rose in the ranks of the Air National Guard, Rita could have let the pressure of being the first woman in key leadership roles shake her hard-earned confidence. All eyes were on her. Would she succeed or fail? Would she end up making women in the military look good or bad?

Rita said she didn't fear failure because she didn't hold herself to other people's standards. By having that mindset, she didn't feel any pressure. In her mind, there was no one to compare herself to because no female had done it yet!

Internal and external pressure to succeed can make people want to quit. Fear of failure can make people not want to try. Let these thoughts and feelings go. Focus instead on taking one step at a time, over and over again.

 Be in command of your own life.

Don't quit, and don't be deterred by obstacles. Do the hard things necessary to level up. Before you know it, you will have climbed to the top of your mountain.

 **TIME TO CLIMB**

Select an idea or goal of yours and write down a specific step you will take within the next week to make incremental, forward progress.

Each week take a new step forward.

KEEP CREATING

You have the power to create unlimited confidence for yourself. The appendix contains 12 additional ways for you to create to create confidence. Read through them all, and see which ones inspire you to action. You can also repeat the actions you've already taken in Step #3. It matters less how you create as long as you keep creating.

Key Points of Step #3: Create to Create Confidence

- Try new experiences outside of your comfort zone
- Create positive habits
- Create something new to you
- Take action on what matters to you

CONCLUSION

When you started reading this book, you may have felt hopeless that you didn't have the confidence to achieve your goals or dreams. You may have felt like you were stuck at a dead end.

Here is the truth:

Dead ends don't exist. There is always another way.

When one road ends, get off that road, drive across the grass, and head in a new direction. If you can't do that, you may need to get out of the vehicle and walk. Not all destinations worth going to have roads that take you directly to them. Sometimes, you must forge your own path, trust yourself to figure things out, and be willing to ask for help along the way. With confidence, you can get there!

This book gives you the three simple steps necessary to create unlimited confidence. They are designed to break you free of the mental chains that prevent you from developing into your full potential. That part of your life is over. You've become this new you that understands confidence is self-trust. By learning to trust yourself, you can move past your doubts and fears and start taking action toward the life you envision.

 Let go of the rope and leave your comfort zone behind.

You began with **Step #1: Create Clarity**. You did the internal work on your purpose and values to clarify what is important to you. You made your own definition of success so you can begin taking steps to live your life and not the life others and society expect of you. You dug deep to figure out who you truly are—your personality, interests, strengths, and everything else that makes you unique and special. Next, you focused on the essence of confidence.

In **Step #2: Create Self-Trust**, you became the person you trust more than anyone else. You accept that you like what you like. You do what you say you will do and stick with something even when it's difficult or uncomfortable. You consistently create a positive mindset that fuels you past fear and self-doubt. When you don't have all the answers, you take action anyway because you're not afraid to fail or be told "no." You view mistakes as opportunities to grow.

Finally, in **Step #3: Create to Create Confidence**, you learned that wishing for confidence gets you nowhere. Confidence comes from repeatedly taking action, trying new experiences, and learning from them. You recognized your talents and capabilities by creating something new or new to you. You created positive habits that increased self-discipline and self-trust and took incremental action toward an important goal. As a result, your confidence comes from within rather than from external sources. You don't need praise or approval from others to feel good about who you are and what you do. You also know how to self-generate confidence, which means you will never run out of it.

 You have the ability to create unlimited confidence.

Confidence ebbs and flows. Even confident individuals will have times or days when they don't feel as confident about themselves. Doubt and fear will try to knock them down and destroy the self-trust they have built. That is why confidence is a self-renewing process. You must use your confidence to correct the voice in your head that tells you, "I can't do it" or "I'm not good enough." You know better than to listen to that voice because you have a vision you are committed to making come true.

When you need to self-generate more confidence, come back to this book like you would revisit a dear friend. Go to the sections that energized and inspired you, or re-read the parts you may have skimmed. Go back through the Time to Climb activities. They will inspire new thoughts and ideas in you because you will be further along in your confidence journey. Read and reflect on what you wrote down in your notebook or journal. Do these things to create more self-trust and maintain a high level of self-trust.

Your goal is continuous improvement. Growth isn't always linear. It can often feel like two steps forward and one step back, but if you keep moving forward, you will always be ahead of where you started. That is progress! Even a one percent improvement each day is a success. Keep going, and you will find yourself at the top of your mountain.

Whatever you do, don't quit. You're worth it. Your dream is worth it. If you want it or need it, don't hesitate to hire a coach to help you get to where you want to go. You don't have to walk this journey alone. A coach can provide you the extra guidance, support, and accountability you need to achieve your goals faster and easier. There's a good reason why many successful individuals have coaches.

Also, don't be deterred by setbacks. When something doesn't work for you, it only means you need to try it again or try something else.

 Experience builds confidence. Find what works for you and do more of it.

As you gain more experiences and learn from them, your confidence seeps into every part of your being. Before long, confidence is an integral part of who you are and how you live life. You wanted confidence, and now you have it.

 By taking charge of your confidence, you take control of your life.

You have always been in the driver's seat, and now it's time to arrive at your destiny. With your newfound confidence, nothing will stop you from being authentically you. You can write your own story and create your own happy ending.

By believing in yourself, you inspire others to believe in themselves too. Nothing is more powerful than leading by example and showing others what is possible. Confidence—pass it on.

Thank you for letting me be part of your confidence journey. There is no higher honor for me than to help individuals gain the confidence to achieve their dreams and become the best version of themselves. May the confidence you create for yourself lead you to let go of the rope and say "Yes!" to new adventures and opportunities.

CONNECT WITH ME

Are you looking for continued help and support on your confidence journey?

You can find additional resources on my website *www.CreateUnlimitedConfidence.com*. There you can find a self-trust assessment, watch a video on transformational confidence coaching, and learn how to join an online community where you can connect with me as well as other individuals who want to live life with confidence.

APPENDIX:

MORE WAYS TO CREATE TO CREATE CONFIDENCE

GET A COACH

Sometimes your will and motivation won't be enough to get you to your goal. You tried to do it on your own, but now you feel frustrated, helpless, and stuck. You have too many doubts or giant roadblocks to overcome by yourself. You want to give up because it feels like you're not progressing, and you don't know what else to do.

If you're losing hope and motivation to keep working toward your goal, it's time for outside help from trained professionals. You don't have to struggle alone.

 A proven way to get past feeling stuck is to hire a coach.

There are different types of coaches, such as executive, life, and confidence coaches. All coaches have one thing in common—they are there to help individuals create greater self-awareness, move past barriers, and take action steps to reach their goals.

Grow Self-Awareness

When people have thought or done the same things for a long time, they often don't realize how it's affecting their life. Examples could be self-limiting beliefs about money or ineffective ways of dealing with conflict. Coaches can help map out someone's thought patterns and help them process their emotions around certain long-held beliefs and habits.

Other times, people don't recognize how certain behaviors are being perceived by others and how it's harming their opportunities or relationships. An example of this is a person's verbal and non-verbal communication style. A person may consider themselves a strong and trustworthy leader, and they feel frustrated that others don't view them the same way. They don't realize that how they present themselves to others tells a different story than what they intend.

Coaches shine a light on their clients' mindsets and choices to help them better understand their patterns of thinking and behaving.

Once self-awareness and clarity have been achieved, people can start making conscious decisions that will get them closer to the life they want.

Receiving coaching is a form of personal and professional development. The Institute of Coaching cites that 80% of people who receive coaching report increased self-confidence, and more than 70% of individuals who receive coaching benefited from improved work performance, healthier relationships, and more effective communication skills. Coaches also help individuals gain clarity. For those who say, "I don't know what I want," coaches can guide them in creating a clear vision for their life and assist in goal setting.

Move Past Barriers

Barriers stop people from starting or progressing toward their goals. Not enough money, not enough time, lack of skills, and lack of confidence are just a few of the barriers that stop people in their tracks.

Coaches empower their clients to overcome barriers, whether it's by removing them, pushing past them, or going around them.

They use the coaching process to get people to view their problems from new and different perspectives so they can see possibilities and choices instead of limitations. They guide clients in brainstorming solutions and deciding on a plan for moving forward.

Take Action Steps

A vision can only become a reality through action. Coaches are skilled in helping people commit to their vision and implement their decisions. They empower their clients to close the gap between where they are now and where they want to be. By working with a coach, individuals do the necessary internal work to be ready and willing to commit to the action steps they've chosen.

Coaches serve as an accountability partner and support system in helping individuals make steady progress towards their goals.

A wrong assumption is believing that coaches are only for people who are already successful and have impressive job titles. Coaching is for anyone who wants to improve their career, relationships, or personal life.

Hiring a book writing coach helped me achieve my goal of writing a book in less than 12 months. My coach gave me with the guidance and moral support I needed to tackle such a large project. I wanted the help of an expert so I could create my best work and avoid unnecessary mistakes. Coaching worked! Here you are, reading my published book.

I could have written this book on my own, but it would have been a lot more frustrating and taken much longer. I definitely wouldn't have felt as positive and confident throughout the process. My weekly meetings with my coach kept me motivated, accountable, and focused. Having someone I could trust to talk to about my thoughts, ideas, and concerns made the process enjoyable instead of daunting and stressful. I never felt alone writing my book because I had my coach by my side.

My coaching experience is not unusual. It's the norm.

Coaches help people achieve the results they want quicker and easier and could be the exact thing you need to get yourself across the finish line.

If you can achieve your goal on your own, that's wonderful. Keep going! But if you're stuck, it's time to try a different approach.

It's time to consider hiring a coach when:

- ☀ A goal seems overwhelming
- ☀ You want to give up on your goal
- ☀ You're letting fear hold you back
- ☀ You don't have a plan for moving forward
- ☀ You need someone to hold you accountable
- ☀ You need a confidante who won't judge you

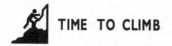 TIME TO CLIMB

Invest in your goals and dreams by working with a coach.

You can get the most out of the experience by being intentional. Begin by answering the following questions:

> *What specific changes or goals do you want a coach to help you with?*

> *What does success look and feel like to you?*

> *What do you need from a coach in terms of support and accountability?*

FOCUS ON CONTINUOUS IMPROVEMENT

Winning in life is not defined by achieving perfection or being better than everyone else. Perfection is unattainable, and comparing yourself to others is a losing game. You can only focus on doing your best every single day.

 You will always be a winner if you focus on achieving continuous improvement.

Making incremental changes and better decisions day after day leads to a better life. When your goal is to be a better version of yourself today than you were yesterday or to get one step closer to your objective, you are competing against yourself instead of others. When you focus on running your own race, you don't waste your time and energy worrying about what others are doing.

You are in control of your thoughts and your actions. Use them to make progress towards your goals and dreams. Progress tells you what you're doing is working, and it builds confidence. Continuous improvement also creates momentum. Things in motion tend to stay in motion. As you make forward progress, things will come faster and easier.

You will only fail if you give up or don't try in the first place. Failure is accepting the status quo and staying in your comfort zone when you want different things for yourself.

Life can be tough, and there will be times when you don't achieve your goal or don't close the business deal. It happens. That's why it's crucial to have the right mindset, like my friend Apollo Woods who said:

> *"Not winning isn't the end of the world because you get experience."*

As a business leader and serial entrepreneur, Apollo doesn't hesitate to get in the game and try innovative ideas. He always gets something positive out of trying. His view of failure is similar to the concept of failing forward. Failing forward means deliberately using failure as a stepping stone to future success by applying lessons learned to improve and try again.

 Make it your goal to continuously improve, and you will make things happen for yourself.

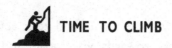 **TIME TO CLIMB**

Live your life like an MIP (Most Improved Person).

In sports, there is a saying, "Play like an MVP." MVP stands for Most Valuable Player. In life, you want to "Live like an MIP" and become the best version of yourself. You are the greatest asset you have. Continually invest in yourself.

> *What can you do to sharpen your mind or create new ways of thinking?*

> *What can you do to develop a new skill or expand your existing skills?*

> *What can you do to improve your physical, mental, or emotional health?*

CREATE A MISTAKE

The process of trying and creating something new can be messy. It involves trial and error, experimentation, learning, and further iterations. Some of them will lead to success, and some of them will lead to mistakes. Mistakes can't be avoided.

Albert Einstein said,

> *"Anyone who has never made a mistake has never tried anything new."*

Mistakes are essential to the learning process. Embrace them. A mistake can teach you something important that you never forget.

Growing up, you were probably warned as a child not to touch hot things because they could burn you. You may remember an adult repeatedly warning you, "Don't touch the stove" or "Don't touch the candle." If you were like me, you did it anyway out of curiosity to see what would happen. It only takes burning your hand once to know not to do it again.

 Mistakes make you smarter.

The American innovator and inventor Thomas Edison created many things in his lifetime. He conducted numerous experiments, and he learned from them. He tested thousands of materials in search of the filament for his most famous invention—the incandescent light bulb. Mistakes did not deter him. He learned from them, which made him confident he would succeed eventually.

"I have not failed," Edison said. "I've just found 10,000 ways that won't work!"

Edison did not base his self-worth on his mistakes, and neither should you.

Inside every successful individual is a powerful mindset. Edison's based his mindset on four principles he lived by:

1. Never get discouraged if you fail. Learn from it. Keep trying.

2. Learn with both your head and hands.

3. Not everything of value in life comes from books—experience the world.

4. Never stop learning. Read the entire panorama of literature.

Edison saw the value in trying, making mistakes, and learning. Trying different things repeatedly led to him generating a record 1,093 patents and changing the world with his creations.

 What would you do if you were confident that you would succeed eventually?

TIME TO CLIMB

Try something that you predict you won't be good at doing.

Show yourself grace and compassion when you make mistakes. They exist to teach you something.

Mistakes become gifts when you learn from them. Journal about what you learned from making mistakes and how they turned you into a wiser person.

CREATE SOMETHING ORIGINAL

When you want to be better at something, trying to copy the people you admire is common. You believe you can have the same success if you can think, look, and act just like them.

Becoming just like someone else might increase your confidence, but only temporarily. Eventually, your confidence will deflate as you realize that you are only becoming a mediocre copy of the original.

Pablo Picasso said, "Good artists copy, great artists steal." He means that good artists try to emulate someone else's style as closely as possible, however, great artists incorporate elements of other artists' work into their own style to create something original.

Original can mean completely new or something that builds on what already exists. It can be a new combination, a new version, or a new perspective. Every person is capable of originality.

 Your confidence skyrockets when you create something original.

There is a sense of achievement and satisfaction in knowing that something came from you and no one else. The more you create original things, the more you start to believe in yourself.

Creation is good for the mind, body, and soul. That is why art is known to be therapeutic. People use it to express themselves in new and creative ways. Dancing to your favorite music, designing a flyer, creating a collage, and writing a story are all forms of original self-expression.

Creating something original will lead you to the profound realization that you are genuinely one-of-a-kind because only an original can create something original.

 TIME TO CLIMB

Stop copying other people and create something that comes directly from you.

It doesn't matter what you create or whether it's "good" or not. Don't judge yourself or your creation, and don't let fear of judgment by others stop you from creating. The power is in the act of creating. Give yourself the creative freedom to express yourself, and see how it changes how you see yourself.

After you create something original, take some time for self-reflection using the following questions:

What feelings did you experience in the process of creating?

What abilities did you use in creating?

What does your creation tell you about yourself?

What will you create next?

GIVE A PRESENTATION

Many people wish they had the confidence to be an excellent public speaker. They want to be able to stand in front of a group of people and speak powerfully and eloquently. They want to be able to stand on stage, tell their story, and inspire audiences to take action.

The mistake is waiting for that feeling of confidence to magically arrive before doing any public speaking. It may never come unless you start practicing in front of people.

 You build confidence in public speaking by giving talks and presentations.

Getting better at public speaking is like learning how to ride a bike. It's awkward at first, but you get better each time. I first started giving presentations using pages of detailed notes. My speaker notes were my training wheels. I felt if I didn't use them, I would crash and burn. My biggest fear was forgetting what I wanted to say and looking like a deer in headlights. My notes made me feel safe. They would remind me of my talking points if I lost my train of thought.

Like training wheels, my notes gave me the confidence to keep trying and improving. Sometimes I fell. My mind went blank on a few occasions, but it wasn't as horrible as I had imagined because it only happened for a moment. I doubt the audience even noticed. Surprisingly, those experiences increased my confidence. Knowing I could recover from losing my train of thought made me less scared of it happening again because I trusted myself to keep going.

 With experience, your confidence will grow and your fears will fade.

With each presentation I gave, my abilities as a speaker improved. I started referring to my notes less and less and connecting with my audience more and more. Then came the day I felt confident enough not to use any notes. I had practiced enough that I was comfortable taking off my training wheels!

Continued practice leads to progression. Soon you've moved to the next level, like learning to ride a bike with no hands. It seems impossible until you learn by doing. With practice and experience, the frightening sensations of being on stage and the center of attention diminish.

Do you remember how you felt the most nervous on your first day of school or a new job? By the end of the week, you weren't as nervous. That's because the newness wore off, and the experience began to feel familiar. Then it started to feel comfortable, if not enjoyable.

A non-profit organization called Toastmasters International helps individuals overcome their nervousness and become better public speakers. They have chapters all over the world that meet weekly. Their meetings give individuals the practice, feedback, and support they need to grow their confidence in public speaking. It's a judgment-free environment filled with people who want each other to succeed. It's a safe space to leave your comfort zone.

Someone told me a story of a Toastmasters meeting when a woman went on stage to give her very first speech. This woman feels extremely nervous, so much so that she can't look at the audience. However, she is determined to give her speech, and the group supports her in doing whatever she needs to feel comfortable enough to do it. The woman ends up giving her entire presentation with the lights turned off and her back to the audience.

While unconventional, she completed her first speech! It grew her confidence because she went back and gave a second speech. The lights remained off, but this time she faced the audience.

 Progress is a form of success, and it comes from taking action.

In another story about Toastmasters, a man is giving his speech and having the most difficult time getting the words out of his mouth. His Toastmasters mentor quietly goes up on stage, stands behind him, and puts his arm on the man's shoulder. That simple act of encouragement gave the man the moral support he needed to finish his speech.

According to Toastmasters District Director JP Bachmann, it takes someone about six speeches to believe they can become good at public speaking. It demonstrates that each presentation contributes to growing a person's confidence and that stage fright isn't permanent. The key is to stick with it and keep giving speeches.

As I've mentioned before, don't feel pressured to figure things out on your own. There are people in the world who can help you. Toastmasters focuses on public speaking, but numerous groups exist to help beginners learn a new skill, sport, or hobby. They provide environments that are supportive to beginners who make mistakes. Find them, and you will not be alone on your journey.

 **TIME TO CLIMB**

Commit to giving a talk or presentation in front of a group.

You can't learn to be good at public speaking simply by reading about it or watching others do it. It's necessary to practice speaking in front of people, even if it's five people. See for yourself how it gets a little bit easier each time you do it.

What should you talk about?

A great starting point is to share information based on your experience that others would find helpful or interesting.

Where should you speak?

Look for opportunities to speak at your place of work, your church, or where you volunteer. Are you a member of a group or organization that holds regular meetings with guest speakers? Offer yourself as a speaker for an upcoming event or be the one who makes the announcements or introduces the speaker. Even speaking for a few minutes in front of a group will give you good experience. It's all about practice, practice, practice.

If you can't find a live audience, pre-record or live stream a video of you sharing information and post it on social media. Speaking to a video camera often gives people the same feeling as talking to a group, which makes it a helpful way to practice public speaking.

PREPARE UNTIL YOU FEEL CONFIDENT

Let's say you have an important speech, performance, or job interview coming up. You are nervous, and the stakes are high, so you want to do your best. You know preparation will be key to your success.

As a professional speaker who gets paid to speak to hundreds of people at a one-time event, I feel pressured to do my best each time. After all, there are no do-overs.

How do I handle that the pressure? I do everything in my power to prepare in advance, and then I assume that things will go well.

 The best results combine positive action with positive thinking.

You may wonder how much preparation is enough? How will you know if you're ready?

Prepare until you feel confident that you will succeed.

Keep practicing until the "I've got this!" feeling finally hits you.

The amount of time and effort that takes depends on the factors of each situation, such as your level of skill or experience going into it. A topic I've presented on before will take less preparation for me to feel confident in presenting again. However, a new keynote may take 10 times as much preparation.

It's necessary that you feel confident going into a situation because it will affect your performance. You are more likely to succeed when your level of preparation leads you to focus on feelings of success rather than feelings of failure.

 When you feel confident, you trust yourself to do your best and that your best will be good enough.

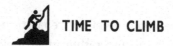 ## TIME TO CLIMB

Pick something you have avoided doing because you needed more confidence.

What are three different things you can do in advance to prepare?

How will completing each action increase your confidence level?

How can asking for help or reaching out to someone who has already found success help you better prepare?

Keep preparing until you feel confident, and then do your best!

FIND THOSE YESES

Once a year, Girl Scouts raise money for their troops by selling a variety of Girl Scout cookies, the most popular being Thin Mints. They hold booth sales at businesses and sell door-to-door. It's a popular fundraiser that teaches girls business skills such as goal setting, sales, and money management.

Katie Francis set two national cookie records as a member of Girl Scouts Western Oklahoma. She broke her first record when she sold 44,200 boxes of Girl Scout cookies in a single season. The average Girl Scout sells about 300 boxes.

Katie sold Girl Scout cookies for 10 years in a row. I'm proud to say I was one of her customers, along with Jimmy Fallon, when she sold him a box of cookies on the hit television show "The Tonight Show." By the time she graduated high school, Katie had sold a lifetime grand total of 180,000 boxes of cookies, earning her the national career record as well.

Katie's accomplishments have inspired other Girl Scouts to follow in her footsteps by setting big cookie sale goals and working hard to achieve them.

She often gets asked, "What is your secret?" According to Katie, she has no secret. She sets a goal, and she goes for it by breaking the goal down into manageable pieces. She does the math to make sure she knows exactly how many boxes she needs to sell every single week. She also makes a lot of asks.

 No one says yes unless you ask them.

Katie learned at her first cookie booth sale that when you ask people to buy Girl Scout cookies, some will say no and some will say yes. In her experience, there are four no's to every yes. How does she deal with that much rejection?

Katie said it's all about "finding those yeses."

She found the tens of thousands of yeses she needed by selling in non-traditional ways. While most Girl Scouts only sell in front of big box stores, door-to-door, and to family and friends, Katie also sold in restaurants, office buildings, bowling alleys, and even gyms. I personally witnessed her successfully sell cookies to people running on treadmills at Planet Fitness! It shows you how committed Katie was to finding those yeses.

Katie knew from experience some people will buy Girl Scout cookies. The customers existed. She only needed to find them.

> *If she kept asking, she trusted herself to keep finding those yeses.*

If Katie had a secret, it would be her mindset. She didn't dwell on the countless rejections she received, and she didn't take no's personally. Rejection could mean a person was on a diet or waiting on a paycheck.

"There could be a billion different factors," she said.

Katie didn't assume their reason for saying no was in any way related to her. Instead, she took the rejections as a learning opportunity. She used them to hone her selling skills, such as getting better at choosing her selling locations in order to maximize her time and sales.

It's all too easy to focus on the negative side of selling— being told no. Katie's strength wasn't that she was skilled at handling rejection.

> *Her strength was that she never gave rejection a lot of thought.*

She focused her thoughts and emotions on the positive side of selling, and for Katie this was the opportunity to engage with the people in her community. She enjoyed meeting individuals and brightening their day. Even though Katie tracked her sales and progress diligently on a spreadsheet, it was about more than the numbers.

For Katie, the Girl Scout cookie sale was mostly about having fun and building skills. That was her definition of success. Reaching her cookie sale goal was a bonus. Katie knew she would still feel good about herself even if she didn't sell enough cookies.

"People are afraid to do things because they assign their worth to it," Katie said. "I don't assign my worth to whether I succeed or fail."

Katie used the confidence she gained from selling cookies to do something she never dreamed of doing. She applied to an Ivy League university during her senior year in high school. She figured her chances of being accepted were very low. After all, she wasn't a legacy, and her family didn't have a lot of money for tuition. In addition, her research on the school made it seem as if an individual had to be the perfect student to get accepted. She knew she wasn't perfect, but she applied anyway.

"I got in because I went for it," Katie said.

She understood the necessity of taking a chance and taking action to reach a goal.

She learned that from selling cookies, and she's not the only one. Hundreds of thousands of girls grow their confidence by gaining real-world sales experience during the Girl Scout cookie sale. As they make ask after ask, they taste the sweet satisfaction of finding those yeses, and they want to keep doing it.

You can also enjoy the sweet satisfaction of finding those yeses. Whether it's selling your ideas, skills, services, products, or personality, it all starts with a single ask. The more you ask, the more you create opportunities for your confidence to grow.

How can your mindset be more like Katie's?
What big goal will you have the courage to go after?

 **TIME TO CLIMB**

Go after something you want by finding those yeses.

Start by finding one yes. Keep asking, and don't let one no or 10 no's stop you from finding the yeses you need to achieve your goal.

CREATE A PERSONA

Sometimes you want people to see a more confident person than the one you feel inside at the moment. This is often the case when you will be rewarded if perceived positively.

When you want people to see a more confident side of yourself, it helps to create a persona that embodies the characteristics of the person you want to be. A persona is a version of you that you want the world to see.

Because it's separate from your daily self, a persona frees you to do things you would never do.

Even before I was a keynote speaker, I went on stage embodying the characteristics of incredible keynote speakers I admired. I walked and talked on that stage as if someone had paid me tens of thousands of dollars to be there. Having that persona in my mind pushed me to behave like a top-notch speaker even when I didn't see myself that way.

A persona helps you visualize the person you know you can be and turn that vision into reality.

The one and only Beyoncé used a persona, also referred to as an alter ego, to great success. In 2008, Beyoncé appeared on *The Oprah Show* and shared how her alter-ego Sasha Fierce helped her overcome stage nervousness in order to give her best performance. She said Sasha Fierce comes out when she hears the crowd, puts on her stilettos, and right before the moment she gets nervous.

"Then Sasha Fierce appears, and my posture and the way I speak and everything is different," Beyoncé said.

"It's kind of like doing a movie," she added. "When you put on the wig and put on the clothes, you walk differently."

Creating a persona allowed Beyoncé to perform with a level of confidence she didn't yet have. Beyoncé channeled Sasha Fierce for many years to become one of the greatest performers of all time. Like putting on different clothes, a persona lets you wear a different mindset. The change is significant.

 By thinking differently, you act differently.

A day may come when you no longer need a persona to push you to become the person you want to be. You are no longer "wearing" a mindset. The mindset is you. Your self-identity has evolved to match your vision.

"The thing that's interesting is I don't need Sasha Fierce anymore because I've grown, and I'm now able to merge the two," Beyoncé said. "I want people to see me. I want people to see who I am."

A persona can give you the confidence to do something entirely outside your comfort level. My friend Susan O'Hara suffers from lipedema, a chronic medical condition that causes excess fat to accumulate in the legs and buttocks. She uses her website LegsLikeMine.com to advocate for women with lipedema to improve their lives.

One topic she writes about is swimming to improve her physical health and the bathing suits that fit her body type. When she received an invitation to model her aquatard bathing suit on stage at a lipedema conference, she panicked. It was not something she wanted to do. However, Susan told herself something that gave her the courage to accept the invitation:

"Act like you own the world, and people will believe you, and you will start believing in yourself."

Susan did precisely that. She used her new mindset to become a person who was able to model her bathing suit in front of hundreds of people. As a result, everyone saw a beautiful and confident woman.

A persona will help others see you as confident, but the true power of a persona is that it will help you see yourself as confident.

TIME TO CLIMB

Create a persona or alter ego who can bridge the gap between where you are now and where you want to be.

Describe the personality, characteristics, and mindset of this completely confident version of you.

How does this version of you act when it comes to doing and getting what you want?

What will you name your persona?

USE YOUR VOICE

Have you noticed that some people are more confident than others in speaking up and sharing their opinion?

Everyone, including you, should be confident in sharing their opinion. An opinion is a person's belief, view, or judgment about something or someone, not necessarily based on facts.

 You have a right to your opinion and the right to speak your truth.

Madeleine Albright went from refugee to being the first woman to serve as United States Secretary of State. She was known for her outspoken reputation and ability to tell it like it is because she wasn't afraid to give her opinion or disagree with others.

But she didn't always live her life that way. Early in her career, she felt she needed to be agreeable to please others. But ultimately, she realized she wasn't helping herself or her country by keeping silent.

As Secretary of State and ambassador to the United Nations, Albright was often the sole woman of power in a room full of men. Over time, she learned not to let that bother her, and she showed the world that confidence is not needing an invitation to speak your mind. Albright believed that everyone has a voice and should use it. "It took me quite a long time to develop a voice, and now that I have it, I am not going to be silent," Albright said.

Even after leaving public office, Albright kept sharing her views and opinions with the world through her books, interviews, and opinion editorials in major newspapers. Only her passing in 2022 could quiet her voice.

Like Albright, you are not helping yourself or anyone else by staying silent. Speaking up and sharing your truth takes practice, but it gets easier the more you do it.

What do you have a strong belief about? What is your truth that you want to share or that others need to hear?

 Don't be silenced. Your voice has the power to ignite change.

 # TIME TO CLIMB

Use your voice to speak up by sharing your thoughts or opinions about something important to you.

Speak your mind respectfully and without apology. There is no need to preface your opinion with phrases such as "I think" or "I believe." Simply state your thoughts. If you want others to act on what you say, use power phrases such as "I recommend" or "I propose." If you have a differing idea or opinion to share, say something along the lines of "Another way to look at it is...."

Here are some possible ways to start using your voice:

- Share your opinion about the best bands or top movies of all time.
- Talk about a problem at work and your view on the best way to solve it.
- Pick a hot topic in the news. Do your research and express your informed opinion.
- Pick an issue that has opposing views. Share where you stand and support your opinion with facts.

When sharing your opinion, be prepared for some people to disagree and use it as an opportunity to create dialogue. If someone who disagrees is rude or disrespectful, you must decide whether it makes sense to defend your opinion or walk away. Beware that social media may or may not be the best place for you to share an opinion since unpopular opinions can sometimes result in harassment or personal attacks.

Journal about your experience:

> What was it like to use your voice to speak up about something important to you?

> What did you learn from using your voice?

> What did using your voice do to your level of self-trust?

VIEW THE WORLD WITH OPTIMISM

You can only imagine and anticipate what happens next when you don't have all the answers. Do your mental images of the future energize or stress you out? When there is uncertainty, do you assume the worst or look on the bright side?

Optimism is hopefulness and confidence about the future or the successful outcome of something. It fuels you to take action toward the positive future you see.

 Optimism acts as a shield against negativity, both internal and external.

It fights against the things that will tear down your confidence. When you assume positive outcomes, you don't dwell on fear, doubt, and negative self-talk. Instead, your optimistic attitude makes you believe things will improve and that setbacks are temporary.

Since a person's level of optimism influences their confidence level, it's essential to cultivate a mindset and an attitude that assumes good things will happen.

There is a cartoon picture that exemplifies the type of optimism that is helpful in life. In it, a young girl asks, "What will the new year bring us?" Her cat responds, "365 opportunities."

Everyone has 365 opportunities, but it takes an optimist to see them.

My optimism is one of the reasons I am able to maintain a high level of confidence. I believe the world is a good place, most people are good, and good things will likely happen to me. Equally important, I believe I can increase the chances of good things happening to me with preparation and hard work.

Despite that, I am not immune to self-doubt. When I've filled out applications for scholarships, jobs, or other opportunities, I've experienced feelings of insecurity. I've wondered, "Will they like me? Am I good enough? What if I don't get it?"

It's easy to let my mind go down that dark hole, but I don't. Optimism kicks in, and I tell myself, "My application is strong. I've given it my best shot. I have as good a chance as any of getting it." These are not just words I tell myself. I genuinely believe them.

I once heard the phrase:

*"If you are going to doubt anything,
doubt the doubt and kick it out."*

 **Kicking negativity out creates more space to
find the good in yourself and life.**

 **TIME TO CLIMB**

Create optimism in your mindset and attitude.

Here are some strategies for creating optimism and a pattern of positive thinking:

1) Journal regularly about the good things in your life and what you're grateful for.

2) Notice the good things that happen.

3) Show appreciation for the people you care about.

4) Identify what is in your control, and take action that will cause good things to happen.

5) Surround yourself with optimistic people.

HAVE A DIFFICULT CONVERSATION

Whether it's someone who doesn't keep their commitments or someone who says something that upsets you, you will find yourself in challenging interpersonal situations throughout your life. Often, the only way to improve the situation or move past it is to talk directly with the person about it.

These types of talks are called "difficult conversations" for a reason. They are difficult because of the emotions involved and the natural desire to not upset people and make matters worse. For these reasons, you may be tempted to avoid having difficult conversations.

If you do, you will pay a high price in the form of built-up resentment and diminished self-trust. Don't let yourself down by giving in to your fears. Believe in yourself to do hard things worth doing.

 Increase your self-trust by doing what is necessary and right.

Although it feels like conflict, difficult conversations are opportunities to build trust and respect and create a safe space for dialogue. They can also lead to stronger, healthier relationships.

Based on my experience training organizations and coaching individuals on how to resolve conflict, the following strategies lead to more successful outcomes:

- **Have the conversation when your mind is calm and you are in control of your emotions.**
  - Explosive emotions and personal attacks can quickly derail any conversation. Ensure you are in a mental and emotional place to have the conversation and the other person is too. If a situation is fresh, take plenty of time to process your thoughts and feelings. You should not be attacking, blaming, and criticizing the other person in your head when you try to talk to them.

* **Have positive intentions.**
  - Going into the conversation, your agenda shouldn't be to blame or prove the other person is wrong and that you are right. Your intent should be to increase your understanding of the situation and to help. Make that clear in your words and body language.

* **Assume you don't have the whole story.**
  - There is more than one side to every story. Assume nothing and ask lots of open-ended questions to understand where the other person is coming from. Keeping an open mind and showing compassion for their feelings and point of view goes a long way in building trust. Trust between two people is necessary to create open, honest communication that results in dialogue instead of defensiveness.

* **Look for a win-win solution.**
  - The conversation should focus on the issue and moving the situation forward. Don't rehash past mistakes or events. Direct the discussion towards creating a mutually beneficial solution that will make both parties happy. Approaching the conversation in this way will make it highly likely that both parties can come to an agreement, and the relationship will be stronger for it.

Changing the name of something can change how you perceive it and your willingness to try it.

Instead of calling them difficult conversations, refer to them as necessary conversations because they are necessary to resolve a situation or move past it. They are also necessary for healthy relationships and your mental and emotional health.

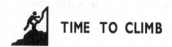 **TIME TO CLIMB**

Schedule to have a difficult conversation you've been avoiding in the next week.

Use the following strategies above to prepare yourself for the conversation. After having the conversation, use the following questions to journal about your experience:

> What was it like to face something you've been avoiding?

> What did that do for your self-confidence?

> What did you do well this time, and what could you do better next time?

> What did you learn about facing your fears that you could use moving forward?

MAKE A POWER PLAYLIST

Music has a powerful way of altering the way you think and feel. The right kind of music can quickly tap into your neurobiological systems to create positive emotions that motivate you into action.

Is there a song that gets you pumped up about life and excited to make your mark on the world?

"High Hopes" by Panic at the Disco is that song for me. When I hear it, my body starts moving, and my adrenaline gets going. It makes me feel alive from head to toe. As the music builds, so does this feeling of power inside me that makes me want to show the world who I am and what I can do. I also love the song because the lyrics speak to my soul about the importance of having a vision and believing in yourself to make it happen.

Excerpt of lyrics from "High Hopes" by Panic at the Disco

> *Had to have high, high hopes for a living;*
> *Shooting for the stars when I couldn't make a killing;*
> *Didn't have a dime but I always had a vision;*
> *Always had high, high hopes*

*   *   *

> *Had to have high, high hopes for a living;*
> *Didn't know how but I always had a feeling;*
> *I was gonna be that one in a million.*
> *Always had high, high hopes*

 Music is an effective tool for increasing feelings of confidence.

Did you know that many famous motivational speakers and performance artists will listen to music right before they go out on stage? The music elevates their mood and energizes them to give their best performance. If music works for many big-time professionals, it can work for you too.

 **TIME TO CLIMB**

Create a Power Playlist of songs that causes you to immediately feel confident.

When putting together your playlist, think of the following:

What song makes you feel happy?

What song makes you feel strong?

What song makes you feel that you can do anything?

What song makes you want to rock out with your entire body?

What song calms your nerves?

What song heals your soul?

What song makes you feel hopeful about the future?

MEET THE AUTHOR

I am Diana.

Diana Rogers Jaeger, APR, M.Ed. is a speaker, consultant, and coach passionate about helping people become the best version of themselves. Confidence is her superpower, leading her to take smart risks and achieve success on her own terms. This book is her way of helping others do the same so they can achieve their biggest dreams.

Diana found her calling as an entrepreneur. She is the founder and owner of Love To Appreciate Consulting, a business specializing in leadership development and employee engagement. She is an expert and a go-to speaker on confidence, leadership, employee retention, and the 5 Languages of Appreciation in the Workplace. Diana attended the University of Oklahoma where she earned a bachelor's degree in public relations and a master's degree in adult and continuing education.

She is committed to building confidence in women and girls. She is a Lifetime Member of Girl Scouts and spent 15 years volunteering for Girl Scouts Western Oklahoma as a troop leader, member of the board of directors, and board president. She currently resides in Fort Collins, Colorado, where she regularly goes camping, hiking, and mountain biking with her husband and two sons. Diana lives and breathes her personal mission statement: "Live a life of adventure while making the world a better place."

Made in USA - Kendallville, IN
10006_9798864570821
04.05.2024 0836